Handbook

of

Intensive

BRIEF and

EMERGENCY PSYCHOTHERAPY
(B. E. P.)
by

Leopold Bellak, M.D.
Clinical Professor of Psychiatry
Albert Einstein College of Medicine / Montefiore Medical Center

Clinical Professor of Psychology / Post-Doctoral Program in Psychotherapy
New York University

and

Helen Siegel, M.A.

C.P.S., Inc.
P.O. Box 83
Larchmont, NY 10538

Library of Congress Catalog Number: 83-20947

Printed in the United States of America

Cover Design: Robert Grossman

TABLE OF CONTENTS

FOREWORD

PART I – GENERAL PROPOSITIONS

1. Overview 1
2. The Ten Basic Tenets of Intensive Brief and Emergency Psychotherapy (B.E.P.) 6
3. The Basic Outline 15
4. The Initial Session 19
5. The Second Through Sixth Session 31
6. The Therapeutic Process 36
7. Methods of Intervention 44

PART II – SPECIFIC CONDITIONS AS PARADIGM

I. Depression 50
II. Acting Out 60
III. Suicide 68
IV. Enabling Conditions for the Ambulatory Psychotherapy of Psychotics 75
V. Acute Psychotic States 85
VI. Physical Illness or Surgery 92
VII. Catastrophic Life Events 104
VIII. Phobias (and Anxiety Hysterias) 117
IX. Panic 127
X. Feelings of Unreality of the Self and of the World 136
Appendix 146
References 162
Index 167

The original idea of a handbook was of a book small enough to be held in one's hand — to be handy. That is the purpose, literally and figuratively, of this book: we want it to be handy in format and content.

L.B.
H.S.

The authors wish to thank Dr. Saul Scheidlinger for his constructive suggestions concerning the manuscript — and for his friendship.

FOREWORD

This Handbook hopes to make the basic principles and techniques of brief and emergency psychotherapy so simple that even people who do not enjoy reading regular textbooks will find it easy and comfortable to use. Ten of the most frequent psychogenic conditions brought to the clinic and private office are discussed in a systematic fashion.

For each condition in Part II, ten factors are first listed. These might be suitable for memorizing or keeping in front of one while interviewing a patient, for instance, one presenting with a depression. Each of the ten variables is then discussed, be they dynamic factors to be kept in mind or methods of intervention.

From the ten major conditions discussed, it will not be difficult to extrapolate treatment of some conditions not mentioned in this text.

While extensive theoretical and clinical knowledge of the experienced clinician will make the perusal of this small publication easier, it should be a useful frame of reference even for less experienced clinicians. It should prove of special value to the psychiatric resident finding himself perplexed in the emergency clinic, or the social worker and the clinical psychologist facing the innumerable problems which they meet every day, both diagnostically and therapeutically.

Since a clear focus, concise conceptualization and parsimony in intervention are crucial for brief psychotherapy to be effective, the attempt has been made to organize the Handbook with these factors in mind.

One interview with a few comments is appended for demonstrating an intake interview concretely. Naturally, one interview cannot demonstrate the broad spectrum of problems and technique, and is bound to have marked shortcomings — as this one does.

In conducting teaching seminars, I have found video-tape demonstrations of different patients, and several sessions of the same patient, invaluable. The video technique permits one to stop at crucial points to discuss and formulate the process. Such a teaching method greatly enhances the learning of B.E.P.

In presenting B.E.P., I want to emphasize the feature which separates it from virtually all other methods of brief therapy: It developed in the context of community psychiatry and community mental health and *it is based on the needs of community mental health.* It is, therefore, designed to be of at least some use with *any* condition or problem on the broad stage of the human spectacle. It can deal with severe chronic conditions, as well as with acute emergencies or relatively minor problems. *What is important in dealing with the specific complaint which brings the patient to our attention is the understanding of the total person.*

Understanding the total person helps one design techniques for *some* help with *any* problem of *any* person. It was said of one old village doctor: "He's a doctor for the healthy. God help the sick!" He is definitely not the model for B.E.P.!

L.B.

1.
OVERVIEW

A Few Historical Remarks:

My particular approach to brief therapy developed in response to existing needs. In 1946, immediately following the war, the Veterans Administration allowed patients to see its contract psychiatrists for only three times on a private basis. Later, the number of sessions was increased to six (and eventually, indeed, to multiples of this basic figure). I wanted to help these veterans, even in the limited period of three or six sessions, and I tried to devise some method of psychotherapy that would make more of a contribution than merely offering reassurance, support or advice; and indeed, in many cases, it seemed that I was able to do just that. At this time, I had already had considerable training in psychoanalysis in Vienna and in this country and I had sharpened my concepts at the Harvard Psychological Clinic (2) (15), and had learned psychotherapy with psychotics at St. Elizabeths Hospital in Washington, D.C.

Beginning in 1948, I was the only psychiatrist at ALTRO, then a rehabilitation agency for tubercular, cardiac and four years later, primarily for psychiatric patients. Being the sole psychiatrist for all these patients, I attempted to make use of what I had learned from my prior work with veterans and developed more specificity, i.e., in the care of post-cardiac patients and chronically ill tuberculars and later neurotics and psychotics. In fact, in 1952, I published my first paper on brief psychotherapy in the context of emergency psychotherapy of depression (3).

In 1958, while I was the director of the Department of Psychiatry at Elmhurst City Hospital, I developed the Trouble-Shooting Clinic, which was actually the first psychiatric walk-in clinic in the United States, fully staffed and operated 24 hours a day. It soon became an integral part of the hospital as a Community Mental Health Center. A few years later, the Community Mental Health Act of President John F. Kennedy made such clinics a standard fixture in most Community Mental Health Centers. At this time, I also started what was possibly the first placement of mental health professionals in a medical/surgical emergency clinic (18). I continued honing my technique of brief therapy in all these settings, and NIMH funds made it possible for me to engage in intensive as well as large scale research in the area of brief therapy, all aimed to validate it as a method of therapy (16) (49).

The foregoing history is relevant to the understanding and rationale for my method of brief intensive psychoanalytically oriented psychotherapy (B.E.P.): the method was a pragmatic response to the limited resources offered

1

to WWII veterans. My time limitations in caring for patients at ALTRO was a further determinant of this method, while the Trouble Shooting Clinic at Elmhurst was at the time virtually the only dynamically oriented facility available to the Queens population of two million. From these realities derives an approach which tries to be of help to the greatest number of those in need. It clearly differentiates from short-treatment methods that pre-select suitable patients, such as the STAPP approach of Sifneos (54) or those who offer excellent but relatively lengthy therapies, like the 30 sessions of Malan (38), or therapies with a theoretical limitation, like those of Mann (39), which primarily limits itself to the treatment of separation anxiety. Similarly, the confrontational method of Davenloo (22), in my opinion, is likely to be more than some very disturbed patients can bear, leave alone the fact that most out-reach programs as well as private practitioners would be unable to afford the routine videotaping intrinsic to his approach.

In essence, then, though there is merit to other approaches to brief therapy, my particular approach is a broader attempt to deal with any and all problems brought to a clinic, an office, or a sick room. This approach is primarily based on psychoanalytic theory, but also borrows from learning theory and systems theory. Speaking of systems theory, for example, to understand an agoraphobic patient it may be important to understand the family oriented attachments of an Italian patient as compared to one from some other ethnic group, or alcoholism in an Irish patient, or drug dependence in a Puerto Rican in New York, or the need for achievement in the first born male in an immigrant Jewish family.

If a vicious marital battle brings a couple to the Emergency Clinic, I can't offer each of them psychoanalysis, as some of my purist colleagues would suggest, nor can I exclude them if they aren't ready to engage in Anxiety Arousing Therapy, nor can I offer them 30 sessions of therapy or discuss only their separation anxiety. Instead, I have to start with the under-standing that the husband's recent job loss has precipitiously lowered his precarious self esteem, also increasing his tendency to be jealous. In his particular ethnic setting, this especially threatens his systems status as the "pater familias." Understanding this, my interventions will have to address themselves directly to these problems. Given a few sessions, the husband may be able to relate his difficulties with self-esteem regulation to his childhood history with regard to the sibling series, as well as relating his present jealousy to primal scene problems when he shared the parental bedroom. Couched in appropriate language and style, some such interventions may indeed then go beyond just quieting the immediate situation and may at least initiate a few modest structural and dynamic changes, which, in my experience, have some-times lasted for years. On the other hand, for some patients for whom such insight would not be possible or tolerable, conjoint therapy with an emphasis on behavior modification, based on *my* dynamic understanding and insight, may be the method of choice.

I once treated a car mechanic who appeared at a medical clinic with a fear of dying from a heart attack. We were able, in five sessions, to work through dynamic problems, such as his excessive dependency on his over-protective mother. This patient responded to brief therapy well enough to return to the clinic only ten years later, when similar circumstances caused a brief relapse. Even after the elapsed 10 years, the patient was able to utilize insights he had gained a decade ago.

Another patient seen in a liaison psychiatry context, in a panic over an imminent surgery, was helped to explore his apperceptive distortions, which made him view the operation as more frightening than need be. Classical castration anxiety [which I of course relayed to the patient in suitable terms and style (to be discussed more fully in a later chapter)], fear of passivity and loss of control under anesthesia, were successfully ventilated in five sessions. Education of this patient with regard to the surgical procedures involved, as well as to the post-operative expectations, provided a great deal of relief and probably a patient with a better prognosis.

Essentially, I would delineate my approach to Intensive Brief and Emergency Psychotherapy (B.E.P.) as follows:

1. *Intensive B.E.P. focuses on the crucial features of the presenting disorder.* I thus attempt to find the best vantage point from which to understand the patient sitting in front of me. As a psychoanalyst, I have found broadly conceived psychoanalytic theory of personality, of psychopathology, and of treatment, most useful in terms of understanding (seeing casual connections), of predicting, and of controlling behavior (in a therapeutic sense). This psychoanalytic orientation does not preclude a systems theoretical or cognitive approach, nor does it preclude behavioral therapy rather than insight therapy, when I feel the former is indicated. All I insist on is that one *understand the patient as fully as possible from all vantage points,* and then introduce the variables which will make for the most efficacious adaptation.

2. In all instances, *I attempt to establish a focus by understanding precisely why the patient came to see me the particular day he did,* when his problem started in his immediate past, and when and in what similar form it existed in his total prior life history.

3. I see the major contribution of psychoanalysis as the *establishment of causality — of continuity —* between the present and the past, and the many systems theoretical connections in the present. In focused psycho-therapy, *we attempt to bridge the discontinuity between childhood and adulthood, between waking and sleeping thought, between what is conscious and what is unconscious,* as well as attempting to understand the interface of

3

these factors to the biological, social, familial, and physical components of the patient's life.

Above all, I attempt to establish continuity between the presenting symptoms or personality problems and conflicts or/and/defects (in terms of self-representations and object representations), finding both classical analysis and object relations theory valuable and compatible.

The concept of causality, of determinism and overdeterminism, is crucial for focused psychotherapy: Why did a particular symptom, e.g., a panicky feeling that figures were suddenly receding into the wall, develop on a particular evening at 8:15, in the particular reported setting that it did? Why did another patient, a gas attendant, develop the panic that he has about to have a heart attack on a Saturday morning at exactly 10:30? To understand the specificity of symptom presentation, one has to understand all the major forces that coalesce to produce the particular symptom in the specific form that it takes.

4.   The overall most useful formulation of a theory of symptom development, as well as personality structure in general, is that *symptoms are attempts at problem solving, at coping with anxiety, conflict, deficit.* The poorer the coping ability, the more disorder will exist in the personality, and vice versa. Coping behavior is learned, predicated upon a biological substratum and within a social, ethnic, familial milieu. In that sense, to the extent to which behavior is learned, i.e., due to experiential factors, it can be changed by relearning in psychotherapy. Treatment is an attempt to help a person attain better devices for coping with reality, with the conflicts that exist between reality and drives, and with defective introjects (i.e., internalized images of significant others).

5. In that sense, I see all psychotherapy as a form of learning, unlearning, and relearning: *Intensive Brief and Emergency Psychotherapy (B. E. P.) focuses on what has been poorly learned, and what needs to be unlearned and relearned, in the most efficacious manner.*

6. Brief therapy, including brief psychoanalytic therapy, has a consider-history. In fact, it has at times been said that what Freud originally practiced was most often brief psychotherapy. Examples of two famous cases of his wherein he really did practice very brief (and effective) therapy were his treatment of the conductor, Bruno Walter (45) for paralysis of his arm in six sessions and of the composer, Gustav Mahler (34), whom he treated and cured of impotence in a single four-hour session. Freud's use of brief therapy is often cited in an attempt to denigrate brief therapy as nothing more than a return to what Freud did long ago. The fact is, of course, that what Freud did in the early years of the century did not have the benefit of the ego psychology he later developed, or the knowledge of defenses that Anna Freud (25) and others later formulated, nor did it have the benefit of the contributions of Hartman (28) and a host of others in this area.

4

Skilled, Intensive Brief and Emergency Psychotherapy, on the other hand, *proceeds with full accounting for defenses and ego psychological propositions.*

7.   *Intensive Brief and Emergency Psychotherapy (B.E.P.) focuses on — and selects — the main and most disturbing symptoms and their cause, within the broadest possible framework, and then provides the most sharply focused conceptualization* possible of the necessary and hopefully, sufficient, psychotherapeutic interventions.

8. *The essence of B.E.P. does not lie in six sessions, or four or eight, but in the systematic, focused approach.* Five or six sessions may be most practical, because experience shows that most outpatients are not willing to return for more than that, probably based on their experience with medical treatment.

9. *The benefits of B.E.P. may extend well beyond the immediate focus of the therapy,* as the patient's whole adaptative structure may change favorably, in a kind of psychodynamic chain reaction, as a result of the limited interventions.

10. The indications for B.E.P. are very broad. *We select the problem for treatment, not the patient.* In that sense B.E.P. may be used for primary, secondary (acute conditions) as well as tertiary prevention (chronicity) in a wide range of disorders.

Certainly, for some patients, brief therapy, as all therapy, may be nearly impossible or in fact impossible. Thus, very passive patients with little ability for insight, regardless of their symptomatology, may be the most difficult to treat, at least with insight oriented therapy. Based on an understanding of the patients' dynamics, however, they may be treatable via some other modality, i.e., supportive therapy, behavior therapy, education or environmental restructuring. Some patients, of course, cannot be helped by either brief or long-term therapy. For these, amelioration or symptom removal with drug therapy may have to be the limited goal.

2.

THE TEN BASIC TENETS
of
INTENSIVE
BRIEF AND EMERGENCY PSYCHOTHERAPY
(B.E.P.)

THE TEN BASIC TENETS

of

B. E. P.

1. Intensive B.E.P. relates to traditional long-term therapy the way a short story relates to a novel

2. Close conceptualization is essential

3. Instead of selecting patients, one selects goals and problems

4. Intensive B.E.P. is based on an exhaustive history, guided by clearly formulated concepts, using a suitable style of communication

5. People with relatively limited knowledge of psychodynamics can be taught to perform B.E.P. usefully

6. Schematic Guide: the concept of emergency medicine as a paradigm for B.E.P.

7. Emergency psychotherapy is not necessarily limited to symptom removal. Despite the restrictions of time, there may be a chance for the patient to reconstitute on a level higher than the premorbid one

8. Effectiveness for primary, secondary and tertiary prevention

9. Administrative aspects and indications for B.E.P.

10. Role of the therapist and resistance to Intensive B. E. P.

1. Intensive B.E.P. relates to traditional long-term therapy the way a short story relates to a novel

As a modality, I see B.E.P. relating to traditional therapy the way a short story relates to a novel. Each genre has its own merits and each needs its own expertise. Those of you who appreciate short stories know what a tremendous impact they can have and those who have actually tried to write a short story know what a terribly demanding task it is and certainly nothing that a writer need feel apologetic about. Surely the novel too needs special talents and can offer a rich panoply unequalled by the short story, but the two are not in competition, and each has its own merit and indication. So too does brief therapy require special skill and expertise. The therapist should understand that he is doing valuable work and not just taking stopgap measures.

2. Close conceptualization is essential

The basic proposition for brief therapy is that it is important to understand all, to know a great deal, and to then do the one thing that will make the crucial difference.

One of my favorite stories involves a general whose car broke down on maneuvers. When none of the army mechanics were able to fix it, an old village smith was asked to help. He lifted the hood, examined the engine, and then gave the distributor cap a sharp blow with his fist. Immediately, the motor started up. The general asked, "What do I owe you?" The village smith replied, "A hundred bucks." "A hundred bucks for one bang?" asked the general. "No," replied the smith, "One buck for the bang, ninety-nine for knowing *where* to bang."

That's the way I see B.E.P.

To accomplish this, one has to do a great deal of thinking, planning and conceptualizing. It is this close conceptualization that makes brief therapy possible.

3. Instead of selecting patients, one focuses on goals and problems

I do not believe it is necessary to specially select patients for brief psychotherapy. That process leaves too many by the wayside. Instead, goals should be set in each particular case. For instance, brief intensive therapy may be useful for some *chronic psychotics* if success is defined as enabling them to remain in the community without being hospitalized or return to work after an acute flare-up of their illness has necessitated their hospitalization. It is not expected that brief psychotherapy will cure a severe *character neurosis*, but it is often possible to change the most distrubing feature of such a neurosis or some particularly disruptive symptoms. Moreover, acute anxiety attacks or depressions and many other acute conditions do lend themselves successfully to brief therapy.

I suggest that *brief therapy be considered the first method of choice*, and only when brief therapy fails or when there is reason to desire more extensive changes should long-term psychotherapy or psychoanalysis be employed.

4. Intensive B. E. P. is based on an exhaustive history, guided by clearly formulated concepts, using a suitable style of communication

Fundamentally, B.E.P. works from an understanding of the patient in terms of his history, his current life situation, his ethnic and cultural milieu, his total human experience, and whatever can be learned about his "Anlage" and general predispositions. I conceptualize this combined information psychoanalytically and help the patient in relearning and restructuring with the help of a therapeutic alliance, a treatment contract, and a set of technical interventions. The technique is predicated on a carefully formulated, almost codified, series of interventions. [History-taking will later be discussed fully under *The Initial Interview* (See Chapter 4)].

To summarize, *brief intensive therapy must involve a complete anamnesis, as complete a psychodynamic and structural appraisal of the person as is feasible, and a consideration of the social and medical aspects.* Then, on the basis of the maximum possible knowledge and understanding of the patient, one must actively plan the areas, methods, and sequence of the areas and methods of intervention.

5. People with relatively limited knowledge of psychodynamics can be taught to perform B. E. P. usefully

Theoretically, it would be optimal if Intensive Brief and Emergency Psychotherapy were performed by well-trained clinicians, and preferably well-trained psychoanalysts. The only disadvantage to this is that the personality acquired in doing psychoanalysis for many years might come to stand in the way of the type of activity needed in brief psychotherapy. But surely to have vast clinical knowledge would indeed be an advantage. Nevertheless, people with relatively limited knowledge of psychodynamics can be taught to perform brief psychotherapy usefully.

The analogy I keep in mind here is that of the role of a paramedic in emergency medicine. Without having gone through medical school, he or she can be taught the fundamentals of physiology and other basic aspects of medicine. In many instances, especially if he has acquired experience, he may be able to perform some emergency procedures better than the average physician because of his specialized knowledge. Similarly, a person specifically trained in B.E.P. may be more effective than someone more broadly trained but without specific knowledge and principles of brief intensive therapy.

9

6. Schematic guide: the concept of emergency medicine as a paradigm for brief intensive therapy

I like the concept of emergency medicine as a paradigm for brief and emergency psychotherapy. Emergency medicine is predicated upon the pragmatic use of a vast body of general knowledge of anatomy, physiology, pathology, surgery and medicine. Emergency interventions are, in fact, more closely defined and conceptualized than other branches of the medical field. Take for instance, the matter of cardiac pulmonary resuscitation. As it is taught to members of the faculty every year by medical technicians, there are some precise and definite steps:

1. If patient is unconscious, open airway: neck lift, head lift
2. If patient is not breathing, begin artificial breathing: four quick full breaths. If airway is blocked, try back blows.
3. Check carotid pulse
4. If pulse is absent, begin artificial circulation: depress sternum 1½ to 2"

In a way, I'll be basing some of my concrete suggestions for the management of certain frequently occurring, frequently presenting psychiatric conditions, on this emergency medical model.

7. Emergency psychotherapy is not necessarily limited to symptom removal. Despite the restrictions of time, there may be a chance for the patient to reconstitute on a level higher than the premorbid one

To my mind, the principles of B.E.P. are the same as those of emergency psychotherapy, except that in brief therapy one may have to define the goal, while in emergency psychotherapy the goal is clearly defined by whatever presents as the emergency, be it a suicidal danger, homicidal danger, a panic attack or some other crisis. In the literature, some have differentiated between emergency therapy and crisis intervention (43): they hold that in crisis intervention, the main goal is to restore the patient to a pre-crisis state without any attempts to attain a higher level of resolution and functioning. It has become quite clear to me that in the process of resolving a particular situation, patients often, even with the briefest therapy, reach a generally higher level of problem solving and also have the advantage of having acquired something akin to a vaccination, some strength from having survived a particular situation that will provide them with some immunity for the future.

For brief therapy to fulfill its promise as a treatment modality useful for and available to the greatest number of people, it must be a technique that is suitable for any circumstances.

With regard to attaining higher levels of problem-solving, I want to remind you that the Chinese symbol for crisis means danger plus (+) opportunity, and in this case *the danger offers the opportunity for a better re-integration.*

In crises and emergencies, it is important to realize that patients in crisis often suffer from a kind of tunnel vision, as I will discuss particularly with regard to suicidal danger. They can often perceive only a very narrow spectrum and often only two alternatives. Very often, one of the first tasks in converting a crisis or emergency situation into a more manageable situation is to help the patient have a broader view than his tunnel vision would grant, and to be able to see his alternatives and options.

Especially in these days of budgetary restrictions, many people feel rather cynically that brief therapy is a cheap substitute for long-term therapy. The fact is that brief therapy has a legitimate useful indication of its own, quite independent of financial resources, and I practice it at times with private patients who can well afford long-term therapy. This is not to deny that matters of manpower and financial resources do enter in. At times, brief therapy is all that can be offered, even where long-term therapy might be preferable.

8. Effectiveness for primary, secondary and tertiary prevention

Brief psychotherapy may be useful for *primary prevention* in a great variety of circumstances. When people are at risk psychologically, brief psychotherapy can be used to work through the problems in advance, that is, preventively. For instance, patients facing major surgery or bereavement may benefit from brief preventive interventions. People who have been exposed to violence in the form of rape or mugging may also be helped preventively before they even realize that they have a psychological problem, by helping them work through the impact while they are still in the process of denial or shock.

Secondary prevention deals with already existing acute conditions, which can be kept from developing into more serious and chronic conditions by brief psychotherapy. People who are already acutely disturbed by traumatic events, for instance, would fall into this category.

One example of early secondary prevention concerned a young boy who was brought to an emergency clinic because of bed-wetting and nightmares. His mother related that her younger sister had recently settled with the woman's family and created some imbalance in the family pattern. Her young son, who previously had slept in a small room now occupied by his aunt, had thereupon joined his parents in their bedroom, and in fact shared their bed. This set-up was particularly awkward because he had developed nightmares and occasional bedwetting.

Under the circumstances, I felt it unnecessary to explain the Oedipus complex to her, or the importance of the primal scene. All that was suggested was that the young boy would be better off in a sleeping bag on the kitchen

11

floor than sharing the conjugal bed. It was gratifying to hear that when the change was made, both the nightmares and the bedwetting stopped.

Actually, this case falls between primary and secondary prevention, but it makes the point. The symptoms had not yet hardened into a structure and were therefore easily reversible. Therapists have seen adults who were raised under similar circumstances and who developed a character structure primarily concerned with excessive defenses against passivity, or adapted with homosexual tendencies or fear of homosexual tendencies.

Tertiary prevention has to do with the amelioration of chronic conditions. In psychiatric practice, this means dealing with the acute exacerbations of chronic psychotics, or dealing with their most disturbing symptoms.

It is not generally remembered that a good many chronic psychotics manage to live part of the time in the community, sometimes even fully employed or contributing within their family, but have episodes of acute hallucinations and delusions and panic at various times. Very often, they are then hospitalized for a considerable period of time. Brief psychotherapy can deal with the circumstances that percipated such acute episodes as hallucinations, delusions and other disturbances, and make it possible to either maintain the patient in the community or limit hospitalization to a brief stay.

In one particular instance, a young college student was seen at his third admission to the hospital. He was admitted because of an acute panic that he was going to be killed. He was vague about why and by whom. The history revealed that he had had a very traumatic childhood in which dreams and fantasies about dinosaurs played a marked role. He seemed to have become acutely psychotic around the age of 12, when he was delusionally afraid of dinosaurs doing him harm, and had painful hallucinations of being boiled by cannibals, etc. The current admission, apparently, was related to the fact that a girlfriend had rejected him. This had produced unbearable rage in him and he projected it in terms of somebody trying to kill him, and his old hallucinations and delusions about the dinosaurs and various tortures were revived.

It was possible to work through most of the recent trauma within two sessions: well enough to enable him to return to the community and in fact return to college, while he continued another few therapeutic sessions.

The point is that in this case the patient might have had to be hospitalized for a long time before being able to return to the community, but for a brief psychotherapeutic intervention. Despite the immediate therapeutic success, he remained, of course, a chronic schizophrenic — but a chronic schizophrenic who could live in the community and continue to study, subjectively better off and not a financial burden to the community.

9. Administrative aspects and indications for B.E.P.

Opinions about the appropriate indications for brief therapy vary among different practitioners. Possibly because of my background in the field, I take, in the first place, a community mental health view of it. As Leighton has suggested, "Action on behalf of one must be within the framework of calculations for the many." (35)

I strongly recommend brief intensive therapy as the *intake procedure of choice,* certainly for clinics and social agencies, and I suggest keeping it very much in mind in private practice, even if the patient can afford longer treatment.

For community mental health settings, brief therapy often makes it possible to eliminate long waiting lists and to have people seen quickly, before they develop further chronicity and resistance to therapy. With regard to clinics, there have been statistics suggesting that the average patient will usually not return for therapy more than five times, not being accustomed to the concept of long, drawn-out psychotherapy. Among other things, most people are accustomed to the medical model of usually rather prompt and brief treatment. At the very least, then, I would say that it is better to plan to be as effective as possible within those sessions, rather than to spend practically that many hours of intake only to have the patient not ever return again.

In fact, I see brief therapy as the cornerstone of community mental health.

Some Special Administrative Aspects

There are two possible ways of using brief therapy as intervention in all public clinics: (1) a medical director may see all patients at intake and assign them to the appropriate person; and (2) any available staff member may take the next patient.

Both methods have their advantages and disadvantages. In the former, it is advantageous for the person with, presumably, the most experience to make the initial assessment. Also, if the patient's chosen therapist should become ill, go on vacation, or leave the position, the director can automatically serve as the auxiliary therapist since he has met the patient and has formed some relationship with him. The disadvantage of this method is, of course, the discontinuity: The first relationship is formed with the clinic head and then another must be formed with the therapist. To minimize this break in the therapeautic relationship, the director can call in the therapist at the conclusion of the intake procedure and, in the presence of the patient, review the salient features of the chief complaint, history, and accomplishments thus far. At the end of the presentation, the therapist can ask some questions of the patient and the clinic director; thus, a dialogue is started between the patient and the therapist, and the interview ends with the scheduling of the next session.

If patients are assigned on the basis of therapist availability, the continuity is not broken, and the waiting period, even for walk-in patients, is usually no more than an hour. The disadvantage of this method, however, is that no measures are taken to select the most suitable therapist for a given patient. Also, no one else is directly familiar with the patient in case the actual therapist is unavailable. Above all, there may be a medical disadvantage arising from this administrative structure: Many clinics are organized with one physician as the head, with most of the therapists being psychologists or social workers. If the patient is not screened by the physician in charge, there is a good possibility of a medical condition, which could play a primary or secondary role in the patient's complaints, being overlooked. Medical screening may be a legal requirement in many instances. Furthermore, if the medical director at least has a brief intake acquaintance with the patient, he has a sounder basis for prescribing psychotropic medication if it is needed later than if he only has second-hand information.

10. Role of the therapist and resistance to Intensive B. E. P.

It is important that the therapist not lose self-esteem by his engaging in brief therapy; i.e., he should understand that he is doing valuable work and is not just taking stopgap measures. This point is particularly relevant to therapists trained in psychoanalysis and psychoanalytic psychotherapy. Those trained in dynamic psychiatry and psychoanalysis have learned to respect the patient's statements and to play a receptive, expecting, relatively passive role in therapy. However, *much more mental activity is necessary on the part of the therapist in brief therapy.* While listening, one has to actively conceptualize and plan interventions to a much greater extent than in long-range therapy. One must act on hypotheses, not only by interpretation, but by forms of intervention less often utilized in ordinary dynamic psychotherapy.

This requirement frequently contradicts the training and personality of people experienced in traditional psychotherapy. Not only may they be un-accustomed to the needs of brief therapy, but they may have become psychotherapists and have been able to function well in the field precisely because they were able to tolerate relative passivity. In fact, they may have chosen the profession because of a certain amount of passivity inherent in the maternal role so important in the life of a healer. In other words, an active role often does not come most naturally to them. However, it is clear that a certain amount of therapeutic optimism is useful in attaining therapeutic results, without implying that therapists are simply utilizing suggestion or are carried away by a "Dr. Kildare" syndrome. It is generally accepted that the expectations of the therapist tend to have an influence on the therapeutic result.

3.
THE BASIC OUTLINE
of
INTENSIVE
BRIEF AND EMERGENCY PSYCHOTHERAPY
(B.E.P.)

THE BASIC OUTLINE
of
B. E. P.

1.   Five or six sessions of 50 minutes, usually once weekly

2.   Follow-up session a month later

3.   Complete anamnesis

4.   A psychodynamic and structural appraisal

5.   Consideration of the social and medical aspects

6.   Plan for areas of intervention

7.   Plan for methods of intervention

8.   Plan for sequence of the areas and methods of intervention

9.   Decision as to dyadic therapy only, or whether to be combined with conjoint or family sessions

10.   Consideration of enabling conditions such as drugs or brief hospitalization

The basic outline, as all propositions in this volume, *is meant as a guide, not a straightjacket.* The various steps are only briefly touched on here because most of them are later discussed extensively in more specific contexts.

Five sessions are suggested because this number seems to suit the majority of patients and, in my experience, has worked well. The sixth one, as discussed later, is a follow-up session.

Fifty minutes duration is suggested because I have used it for the last forty years, have found it useful and have become accustomed to it; it seems the necessary and sufficient amount of time. Neither the number of sessions, nor their arrangement or length is immutable. In patients with a panic, one might want to see them more than only once a week. Some patients may need eight sessions. Others may find a 50 minute session too lengthy, while some obsessive patients will hardly get started in fifty minutes and, at least for the initial contact, a double session may be useful and indicated.

Complete anamnesis and dynamic and structural appraisal are discussed in detail in the Initial Session, below.

The social, ethnic, economic and general systems theoretical considerations are very important. They determine the style of communication to be kept in mind with regard to what is pathological and what is within the norm for a particular patient. These factors may determine the forms of intervention (e.g., whether the collaboration of a religious representative is indicated) and they also help to understand the pathogenesis.

Medical aspects have to include the consideration of a series of medical conditions which may represent themselves as psychiatric problems, or which may complicate the psychiatric picture. Street drugs as well as prescription drugs, toxic conditions, neurological conditions, or premenstrual factors may need to be considered as part of the overall picture.

Areas of intervention, methods of intervention, and the sequence of areas and methods of intervention will vary from patient to patient, even if they suffer from the same condition manifestly. In one acting out patient, the first area to be addressed may be his aggression, which should be intervened in with interpretation; another acting out patient's first area may be his feeling of omnipotence, to be addressed by bargaining for a delay. This plan for areas and methods of intervention has to remain flexible, and must be revised as one gains more knowledge and specificity with regard to the patient.

Part of the plan for intervention is the decision as to whether the patient is most suitable for dyadic therapy exclusively, or whether this person would profit from conjoint therapy with an important other in his life, at least for one or two of the five sessions, or whether the patient would profit most from a session with his entire family present.

My use of drugs as enabling conditions for the psychotherapeutic process rather than primarily or exclusively for "target therapy" will probably meet with the disapproval of some psychopharmacologists. I discuss drug use **more** specifically in a number of subsequent sections. The viewpoint, however, persists that the effect of neuroleptics and anxiolytic drugs and antidepressants has to be understood psychodynamically in each patient's overall therapy.

Some topics such as the use of drugs and hospitalization, the role of interpretation, the role of catharsis, and others are touched upon in various sections of the Handbook. In order not to be too repetitive, they are not discussed fully in each instance. It would be best if a reader would acquaint himself with the entire book to know where to best find elaboration of a given point.

4.
THE INITIAL SESSION

1. Chief complaint

2. History of chief complaint

3. Secondary complaints

4. Life history

5. Family history

6. Dynamic and Structural Formulation: Ego Function Assessment (EFA)

7. Transference

8. Therapeutic alliance } The Three Factors in the Therapeutic Relationship

9. Therapeutic contract

10. Review and Planning

1. Chief Complaint

The first session is undoubtedly the most important one and the one involving the hardest work for both therapist and patient.

I try to get my first impression of the patient as I notice him in the waiting room, and preferably for a few seconds before he or she sees me. At that time, the social mask will not have been slipped on yet. I get a particularly good chance to compare the two sides of the face, and the upper and lower halves separately. Discrepancies between the two halves of the face often suggest depression or anxiety or other character traits on one side of the face; these may not be as apparent once the patient is aware of me and which may not be evident if one looks only at the face straight-on as a whole (11).

I am then interested in the patient's gait, his general expression and style. I have formulated some tentative notions about him even before he starts talking. After having introduced myself, I will start off by asking, "What can I do for you?" *I am interested not only in the chief complaint, but in all other possible complaints*, and I will want to know precisely when the current complaint started. I feel that I have begun to understand what ails the patient only if I can clearly relate the onset of his chief complaint and his other complaints to a particular life situation on a given day at a given time.

2. History of Chief Complaint

I then insist on an exhaustive anamnesis. When this remark is delivered at lectures, it frequently occasions some, at best, unbelieving laughter. But I have demonstrated frequently in videotaped sessions that indeed, in one fifty minute hour, one can succeed in obtaining an exhaustive history from the patient, if the interview contains a reasonable and appropriate mixture of spontaneous talking by the patient and the therapist's guiding him towards relevant areas of information. It is this highly conceptualized and structured interview that usually gives me the data I desire.

I conduct a guided interview, i.e., guided by the interlocking hypotheses of psychoanalytic theory. They are a useful frame of reference but should not lead to tunnel vision. If someone complains of an agoraphobia, I will keep in mind that usually separation anxiety, school phobia, unusual ambivalence toward mother and, in women, exhibitionism, are likely to play a particular role, and I will search for the presence of these factors.

In eliciting the history, I especially look for *common denominators* between the onset of the chief complaint and earlier situations in the patient's life. For instance, if the patient suffers from a depression in relation to a loss, I will look for other depressions in relation to a loss in his earlier life, especially childhood, and their possible relationship to the present loss.

In all instances of history taking, one must be informed by theory. In depressions, for instance, I will look for the possible role of the ten factors I

20

consider crucial in depressions (see Part II, Ch. 1). In the case of obsessive complaints, I will look for the role of aggression in conflict with the superego and the defense mechanism of undoing, etc. In agoraphobias, I will search for the pre-oedipal relationship to the mother, and in the case of complaints of premature ejaculation and erythrophobia, I will look for childhood voyeurism, exhibitionism, over-stimulation, bedwetting, etc.

In one patient suffering from acute anxiety, whose treatment I found especially gratifying, I felt satisfied only at a point where I could understand and eventually make clear to the patient, why precisely at 10:30 A.M. on a given Saturday morning, he suddenly experienced the panicky concern that he was having a heart attack.

3. Secondary Complaints

Though the chief presenting complaint may be an anxiety attack or a depression, the patient's secondary complaint may be a long-standing sexual difficulty or an inability to complete tasks or an incapacitating inability to arrive on time. It is important to explore these other areas which may trouble a patient more than he cares to admit and possibly find relationships to the chief complaint.

Interlocking insight may greatly further the therapeutic process.

4. Life History

The best guide I can offer for taking a history is that the therapist should attempt to visualize the person sitting opposite him at different times in his life, especially in childhood, in his actual physical setting within the particular subculture, and in relation to the significant people in his life. Aside from information about the parents, siblings and their respective ages, an attempt should also be made to get some ideas about the prevailing atmosphere in the home. For these purposes, I usually ask that the significant people in the patient's life be characterized by three adjectives.

In each instance, it is very important to ascertain as much as possible about the ethnic and cultural aspects of the patient's life. It is important to see the patient and his problems in terms of systems theory: the family system, the ethnic-cultural system, the socio-economic system.

5. Family History

The nuclear family is the matrix within which a person usually grows up. Therefore, it is essential to understand the characteristics of the family which most likely had a structuring effect on our patient. I say "most likely" because at times a distant relative, a friend of the family, a teacher, a housekeeper or a governess may exert a major influence.

Since time does not stand still, it is important to understand the family setting and the family characteristics at different times of the patient's life. The advent of a sibling may have restructured the family attitudes toward the patient. A job loss on father's part, alcoholism, illness in either parent, any number of factors at different times of the patient's life, may have a major effect. By and large, the earlier the detrimental effect, the more profound an influence it will have on the formation of the personality. It is important to understand whom the patient identified with, both manifestly and latently. The parents' vocation plays a role in the development of the patient's personality. Presumably, a father who worked as a butcher in a slaughter house presents a different image to his growing son than one who peddled Ladies Underwear for a living.

The extended family may play a role in the patient's personality structure, especially in certain ethnic groups where the grandparents often live with the patient and his or her parents.

The medical history, as well as the psychiatric history of the patient's family, is important. Whether or not schizophrenia or the manic-depressive disorders have a genogenic aspect — are or are not transmitted by genes — the environmental effect of people in the patient's life afflicted with one of these disorders is likely to have a major structuring effect. Psychotic siblings frequently frighten the healthy child so much that the result is constriction, because of the fear of loss of impulse control and loss of fantasy control in this healthier sibling. Attentional Deficit Disorder seems to have strong familial features and it is important for diagnosis to know whether others in the family showed signs of learning disabilities, and other aspects of ADD.

Suicidal tendencies seem to have a familial nature, often quite independent of depression. In appraising the danger of suicide in one's patient, it is important to know whether this plays a role in the family background.

It is best again to visualize the patient in relation to the family at different stages of his life, to try and understand character and personality formation and psychopathology in terms of problem-solving and coping behavior.

6. Dynamic and Structural Formulation

The dynamic formulation, quite consistent with the term itself, namely "dyna" or forces, deals with the interplay of forces which are responsible for the patient's personality and psychopathology. We appraise the drives and their conflict and interaction with reality, the superego, and the ego. We want to understand the defenses, how well they work, whether they work too rigidly or too loosely or appropriately.

It should usually be possible to state the major dynamic organization of a person in a simple statement. For instance, in the case of a success neurosis, the typical dynamic proposition is that, more often in the case of a man, he had strong oedipal desires for his mother. This aroused anxiety, both with regard to retribution from the father, as well as recriminations from the superego. The forbidden attainment of mother was generalized to a prohibition of attainment of *any* success, and we accordingly find someone who time and again foils his chances in one way or another, or is unable to reach his particular level of optimal functioning.

Object relations theory is seen both as part of dynamics as well as structure. To start with, it involves the relationship to parental and other figures, and their internalization, as well as the internalization of self-representations. These images then become part of the structure of the ego at different stages as well as of the superego and the ego ideal. The difference between structure and dynamics is a hypothetical one, since Rapaport stated quite correctly that "mental structures are characterized by a slow rate of change (46)." This holds true as much for physics, where we may speak of metal fatigue as certain molecular changes affecting the structure of the metal in its performance.

Ego Function Assessment (EFA)

Aside from a consideration of the psychodynamic, developmental, cultural and ethnic aspects of the patient's life, I engage at times in a systematic assessment of 12 ego functions, usually more formally and in greater detail only with more disturbed patients. In those, particularly some poorly functioning psychotics, it is important to conceptualize in this particular way, so as to determine which of their ego functions are intact and which are disturbed, since therapy may often utilize the intact residue. My particular technique of ego function assessment is the result of an earlier research project and is described in detail in the original work on the subject (14).

The table of ego functions and their components will give a brief idea of the concept.

23

TABLE 1 – EGO FUNCTIONS AND THEIR COMPONENTS

Ego Function	Components
1. Reality testing	Distinction between inner and outer stimuli Accuracy of perception Reflective awareness and inner reality testing
2. Judgement	Anticipation of consequences Manifestation of this anticipation in behavior Emotional appropriateness of this anticipation
3. Sense of reality and sense of self	Extent of derealization Extent of depersonalization Self-identity and self-esteem Clarity of boundaries between self and world
4. Regulation and control of drives, affects, and impulses	Directness of impulse expression Effectiveness of delay mechanisms
5. Object relations	Degree and kind of relatedness Primitivity (narcissistic, anaclitic, or symbiotic-object choices) Degree to which others are perceived independently of oneself Object constancy

6. Thought process

Memory, concentration, and attention
Ability to conceptualize
Primary-secondary process

7. Adaptive regression in the service of the ego

Regressive relaxation of cognitive acuity
New configurations

8. Defensive functioning

Weakness or obtrusiveness of defenses
Success and failure of defenses

9. Stimulus barrier

Threshold for stimuli
Effectiveness of management of excessive stimulus input

10. Autonomous functioning

Degree of freedom from impairment of primary autonomy apparatuses
Degree of freedom from impairment of secondary autonomy

11. Synthetic-integrative functioning

Degree of reconciliation of incongruities
Degree of active relating together of events

12. Mastery-competence

Competence (how well the subject actually performs in relation to his existing capacity to interact with an actively master and affect his environment)

The subjective role (subject's feeling of competence with respect to actively mastering and affecting his environment)

The degree of discrepancy between the other two components (i.e., between actual competence and sense of competence)

Reprinted with permission from publisher and authors (Bellak, L., Hurvich, M., & Gediman, H. *Ego Functions in Schizophrenics, Neurotics, and Normals.* New York: John Wiley & Sons, 1973.)

This graph permits easy plotting and visualization of the ego functions. For more detailed information, please see (14) and (12A).

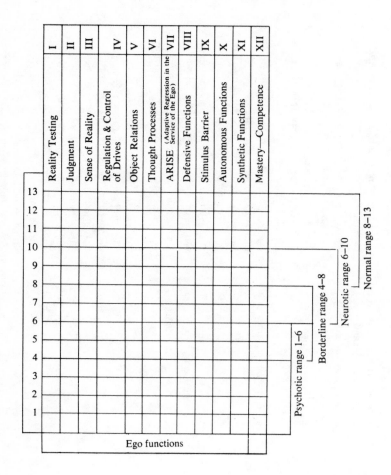

Detailed Ego Function Assessment is useful in the case of very disturbed people, or especially psychotics, where one may have to choose the intact ego functions to shore up the badly affected ones.

Systematic assessment of ego functions is not indicated in the case of neurotic problems.

The Three Factors of the Therapeutic Relationship

7. Transference

In addition to the exhaustive history-taking, I also ask patients, usually at its conclusion, whether they had a dream the previous night, and what dreams they can remember from their childhood; or about recurrent dreams from any period in their lives. I am especially eager to hear about the patient's dream from the preceding night, since there is an excellent chance that it will relate to the impending interview, and may reveal something about the prospective transference relationship and the patient's expectations about therapy, as well as some general dynamics. For instance, if a patient should dream the night before of having to go to the dentist and experiencing a great deal of anxiety and anticipating much pain, it probably indicates one attitude towards therapy, and if he dreams some magic fairy tale resolution to a problem, it would suggest that he has this kind of unrealistic expectation about the therapy.

The dream is an important source, but not the only one, for indications about the nature of the transference relationship. From the history, an attempt must be made to predict what the nature of the transference is likely to be, and what problems can be anticipated. For instance, in some very oral-dependent patients, the excessive wish to be passive and to be taken care of may well become a major obstacle to termination of therapy. If a patient is likely to develop a paranoid transference relationship or an overly sexualized one, it is best for the therapist to be aware of these possibilities in advance. In addition, he has to also check on his own countertransference involvements and monitor them continuously.

It is important to maintain a positive transference in brief psychotherapy and to leave the patient with a positive transference. A negative transference should be analyzed.

8. Therapeutic Alliance

I introduce the therapeutic alliance with a specific formula: *"The rational and intelligent part of you needs to sit together with the irrational unconscious part of you that causes you problems."* I may briefly explain the nature of the therapeutic process as I see it, in the first session, or in the second session, to increase this alliance. I briefly convey some basic ideas:

27

First, that we can understand behavior if we remember that there is continuity between childhood and adulthood, between waking and sleeping thought, and between normal and pathological behavior. I illustrate this fact with an example or two from the patient's account. Dreams, of course, are especially valuable for this purpose by showing the relationship between the day residue, the dream and past history. As noted earlier, the dream might also shed extra light on the nature of the transference relationship.

My second main explanation of the therapeutic process involves an account of the acquisition of dynamics and structure via apperception and apperceptive distortions and role identification. I will compare the experiential process to the laying down of thousands and thousands of transparencies, e.g., of mother feeding, of mother cleaning, of mother punishing, fused with pictures of other significant people in the patient's life and I suggest to the patient that his contemporary apperception of various figures is structured to a greater or lesser degree by these Gestalten acquired in the past.

I may at times use a TAT picture and strive to demonstrate this phenomenon, especially since I tend to use the TAT's sometimes as a device for aiding communication, interpretation, and insight in the process of brief psychotherapy; this is likely to happen in the second or third session. The principle is, of course, that I ask the patient to tell me a story about what is going on in the TAT picture, what led up to it and what the outcome will be, and then I either point out common denominators in his responses or point out highly specific features of his story as compared to some others that I can relate or some specific features such as his not seeing the gun or the pregnancy, etc.

I explain to the patient that the success of the therapy depends to a large extent on the *ability of part of him to work in alliance with me.* So as not to make patients feel overburdened, I may add that their main job is just to talk and that it is mostly my job to lead the way toward trying to understand or facilitate the rest of the process. Many people are, of course, not accustomed to the dissociative process that is involved in good analytic reporting and giving what I call an *internal travelogue.* I frequently convey the idea by relating the story of a delinquent who was being prepared by a social worker for a consultation with me. When she asked him if he knew what a psychiatrist was he said, "Yeah, that's the guy what makes you squeal on yourself." I therefore explain to patients that what is expected is that they squeal on themselves — in a sense, tell things that they observe about themselves. If this is difficult, I have them give a concrete account of their day and then ask them what they thought at different points. I speak of starting with an *external travelogue* and turn next to an internal travelogue. I also have a standard set of questions that help patients report and contribute their part

ERRATA

P. 27 (last paragraph) Change quotation to read, "The rational and intelligent part of you needs to sit together with me, the therapist, so that both of us can try to understand the irrational, unconscious part of you that causes the problems."

P. 28 (third paragraph, line 1) Change ". . . demonstrate *this phenomenon. .*" to "demonstrate apperceptive distortion."

P. 33 (last paragraph, line 2) Change ". . . feel worse the next *time*" to "next *session.*"

P. 34 (third paragraph, line 2) Change ". . . intervening week *was*" to "week *has been.*"

P. 47 (third paragraph, line 2) Change ". . . anesthesia *helps*" to *"aids."*

P. 83 (last paragraph, line 2) Change ". . . the sense *to* self" to "*of* self."

P. 102 (fourth paragraph, line 4) Change ". . . body *organ*" to *"organs."*

P. 112 (second paragraph, line 1) Spelling "catastrophe"

P. 122 (third paragraph, line 7) Change ". . . if the *plan* crashed" to "*plane* crashed."

to the therapeutic alliance. I may inquire as to what they were thinking while engaged in any number of semiautomatic tasks such as driving, shaving, or making up. I may ask them what their last thought was before falling asleep, and what they first thought of upon waking up.

In this respect, I hold myself responsible for *facilitating the therapeutic process,* which does not necessarily mean only making it go. To the contrary, I consider its regulation and flow one of my crucial tasks, analogous to giving gas and putting on the brakes when driving a car. A selective inattention to some material, dilution by a little more general talking, or, on the other hand, silence and interpretation of defenses, are some of the main instruments I can employ to control the therapeutic process as my part of the therapeutic alliance.

9. Therapeutic Contract

Still part of the first session: aside from taking an extensive history and establishing the basics of the transference relationship and the therapeutic alliance, there is also the formulation of the therapeutic contract. As in so many other respects, the therapeutic contract in brief psychotherapy is much more clear-cut and specifically stated than it is in longer forms of psychotherapy. I explain to patients that I hope that we will be able to deal with their problems in five sessions, each of them lasting approximately 50 minutes, and that in all cases I shall want to hear from them about a month after the fifth session, by telephone, letter, or in person, telling me how they are faring. I add that I have reason to believe that five sessions may well be sufficient and successful, but if it should turn out that they are not enough, it will be part of my responsibility to see that the patient gets whatever further therapy is necessary either from myself, or, if that is impossible, from somebody else. I add to this that if I need to transfer the patient to someone else, that second person will be seeing the patient through therapy and that I will personally introduce the patient to the therapist and, with his permission, sit in on the first session, and incidentally, give a brief account to the other therapist in the patient's presence. Of course, I also mention that if there should be a real reason for contacting me before the month is up following the fifth session, then the patient should by all means do so. However, in order to limit the *secondary gains of continued transference feelings and dependence,* I add here that it is best to give the treatment process a chance; I quite genuinely believe that often the treatment process opens up some painful areas which are only partially healed by the time the actual therapy stops. I convey to the patient that it is best to permit the therapeutic process to come to its own conclusion spontaneously and that it is best for the patient to try to give the treatment results a chance to solidify rather than for him to call me the first time anything disturbing is experienced, possibly just because he feels abandoned. I thus try to convey — as part of the contract — that I will indeed continue to be interested and do whatever is necessary but, at the same time, I try to create a situation in which the patient feels motivated to attempt to achieve optimal results in the five sessions — in essence, by my conveying the idea that the *good patient gives up secondary gains and passivity.* Clearly, this is a situation which behavior therapists would consider, appropriately, a matter of reward for giving up some secondary gains. On the other hand, by indicating that I will probably not be the one who can continue the therapy, an element of "punishment" is introduced with the idea of thus being rejected. This factor too may help motivate the patient towards integration.

In essence, this covers the establishment of the three aspects of the therapeutic process in the first session of therapy.

10. Review and Planning

During the manifest and verbal part of the initial session, a silent process that is equally important has been simultaneously at work. While listening to the patient, the therapist should have formulated hypotheses regarding the interaction of genetic, familial, biological, and medical factors with experiential factors within the patient. The therapist should also decide, at this time, on the *best plan of treatment,* such as dyadic treatment, conjoint sessions, family therapy, team approach, use of drugs, use of community resources, etc. If brief intensive therapy is to play the primary therapeutic role, the therapist should *select the areas and methods of intervention and their sequence.* By areas of intervention I mean: In a depression, I may choose to address myself in one patient to the loss of self-esteem and only after that to his aggression, intra-aggression and severe superego. In another patient, I may primarily address myself to his severe superego and the intra-aggression, and turn only later to orality and the feeling of deception and other factors. The method of intervention may be interpretation, catharsis, mediate catharsis, drive repression or others (See chapter 7).

At the end of the initial session, the therapist should review the salient features for the patient. This helps to strengthen the therapeutic alliance. It is also helpful if the therapist can convey, if appropriate, something of the nature of the therapeutic process.

5.
THE SECOND THROUGH THE SIXTH SESSION
of
INTENSIVE
BRIEF AND EMERGENCY PSYCHOTHERAPY
(B. E. P.)

THE SECOND THROUGH THE SIXTH SESSION
of
B. E. P.

Second Session

1. Connect up to first session

2. Thoughts about initial session, dreams, status in between sessions

3. Connect up sessions to maintain focus and increase synthetic-integrative functioning

4. Further explore symptomatology and history

Third Session

5. Special focus on working through earlier insights

6. Start referring to the impending separation

Fourth Session

7. As in other sessions, but more emphasis on termination

Fifth Session

8. Have patient verbally review the entire treatment period

9. End treatment on a positive note

Sixth Session

10. Follow-up Session:
Evaluate the therapeutic achievements and make decision as to whether further work is necessary or not, leaving the patient with a positive transference

The Second Session

In the *second session* we explore further, get better closure, and re-examine the basis for choosing areas and methods of intervention.

I begin the second session by asking the patient how he has been feeling in the intervening week, and eliciting any more complaints that he might have. *I will want to know in detail how he has spent the week*, especially with regard to his complaints. Having paid sufficient attention then to the present and intervening status, I ask the patient whether, by any chance, he had a dream the night after our first session or the previous night. If the patient can report a dream, it usually is very useful in understanding the nature of the therapeutic relationship and the general dynamics of his problem.

I consider it very important to *connect-up between sessions*, especially to have the patient connect-up from session to session. This increases the synthetic-integrative functioning of the ego with regard to the therapeutic alliance.

This session often adds *further historical data* and fills out the dynamic picture. It is one occasion for acquainting the patient with what is expected of him, if insight psychotherapy is the method of choice. I introduce patients to the idea of reporting what is going on in them and increasing their psychological mindedness, their insight, and their ability for awareness — if this seems feasible with a particular patient.

I will discuss other aspects of affecting the therapeutic process (see Chapter 7) but, in essence, as far as the strictly dynamic aspects of psychotherapy are concerned, I see the process here as an attempt to formulate progressively better-fitting hypotheses and establish more continuity for the patient and for myself.

The Third Session

In the *third session* an attempt is made especially at *working through what has been learned so far*, with additions from all possible sources. This may be an occasion for a conjoint interview if that seems the most useful for gathering further information and effecting changes between two people, such as spouses. Or the therapist may feel that a family session would be useful at this point.

From the third session on, I *start referring to the impending separation*. I specifically may state that the patient will probably feel worse the next time and that this might be due to a fear of separation and a fear of abandonment. If this session is a dyadic setting, it should be used to anticipate the termination and to work through separation problems.

The Fourth Session

The *fourth session* is dedicated to understanding more about the patient's problem, adding insights, and intervening in any other way necessary. Again, there will be a *discussion of the termination and reactions to it*. Separation problems play an outstanding role in human relations under any circumstances, and it is especially useful to work them through in such brief therapy.

I try to maintain continuity between all sessions — asking the patient to interrelate them, filling in where necessary, and using this occasion for focusing on specific areas.

The Fifth Session

The *fifth and last regular session* is begun, as usual, by my inquiring of the patient how he is feeling, and how the intervening week was. I then *ask the patient to review the entire treatment period and we work through whatever additional material we have obtained*, especially with regard to termination or other plans.

I aim to terminate with a positive relationship. A "transference cure" is not highly thought of because of its unstable nature. On the other hand, if problems have been well worked through, it is useful for the patient to leave therapy on a note of positive transference, as various analysts have found (42).

As one way of facilitating a positive transference, I change my style slightly in the fifth session, by giving up some therapeutic neutrality and becoming more "human." I engage in some chatting with the patient, perhaps about a shared hobby such as photography, or about a common interest in some current event or sport. I may talk a little about myself or about something I am currently involved with, to decrease the distance of the doctor-patient relationship. I thus try to indicate that, indeed, I consider the patient an equal.

As already noted, my most frequent request is that the patient contact me by telephone or letter at least a month after therapy is concluded, or in person if the patient wishes that. Of course, I am willing to hear from the patient before the month is up, if he should not feel well. However, I try to prevent easy further dependence by pointing out that the termination itself may produce some problems. I point out that if he manages to tolerate the immediate discomfort, it will further strengthen therapeutic attainments. In essence, I give a double message: "I am available if you really need me, but try not to need me because it's good for you if you can go it alone rather than be dependent." At the same time, the patient is again reassured that if it turns out that further therapy is necessary, it will be carried on either by myself or by someone else, whom I will introduce to the patient.

34

The Sixth Session

In the *sixth session*, one month later, I try to *check on the quality of the therapeutic attainments and make dispositions accordingly*. Again, there is an attempt to leave the patient with a positive transference and the not inappropriate feeling that, if need be, I or some substitute will be available to him. Oberndorf (42) long ago pointed out the value of positive transference for the maintenance of good results with often minimal therapy. My own clinical experience, including that with patients seen 25 years ago at ALTRO, bears out the truth of this statement.

6.

THE THERAPEUTIC PROCESS

in

INTENSIVE
BRIEF AND EMERGENCY PSYCHOTHERAPY
(B. E. P.)

THE THERAPEUTIC PROCESS

in

B. E. P.

1. Guiding and controlling the intensity of the therapeutic process

2. Facilitating communication: Appropriate style is essential

3. Explaining the therapeutic process in simplified terms at the end of the initial session

4. Facilitating learning: Appropriate intellectual, conceptual and linguistic style

5. Projective techniques

6. The importance of education: In emergency treatment of emotional reactions to physical illness, have patient sketch the diseased organ

7. Communication between the patient and the therapist

8. Interpretation

9. Insight

10. Working through

1. Guiding and Controlling the Intensity of the Therapeutic Process

To a great extent, B.E.P. can be effective because of the nature and guidance of the therapeutic process. I believe that a therapist must be as much in control of the therapeutic process as is the driver of his car. The therapist must be able to accelerate, apply brakes and steer therapy in the optimal directions. In furthering the process of therapy, I use the method of selective attention or inattention to focus on those areas which I consider appropriate and important. I attempt to regulate the amount of anxiety that a patient feels by increasing it through interpretation of defenses, or decreasing it by a variety of measures, including discussing neutral topics or diluting the atmosphere by relatively decreased intervention. Again, I view this control of the therapeutic process as being analogous to the driver of a car, providing more gasoline or applying the brakes to the car he is driving.

At times, it may be necessary to abandon the position of "therapeutic neutrality" to permit either a more relaxed attitude between two equals or to take the role of the active helper.

2. Facilitating Communication: Appropriate Style is Essential

To begin with, it is the therapist's task to ensure that there *is* a therapeutic process. To that end, he has to make it possible for the patient to contribute his part to the therapeutic alliance. For dynamic psychotherapy, this means, above all, that the patient be able to communicate. Usually, I have to introduce patients to the concept of self-reporting. I already related the story of the delinquent who thought of it as "squealing on yourself." I sometimes tell a variant of Freud's story about two people in the railroad car, one sitting near the window and able to look out and the other sitting on the inside and unable to see the landscape. The passenger near the window has a perfect view, but is unfamiliar with the landscape. The passenger away from the window and unable to see any of the scenery is very familiar with the particular area through which they are passing. The two men make a contract: They agree that the man at the window will call out whatever he sees, and the man inside will then try to piece together what their location might be. The man at the window says, "I see a small village square with a monument to the left and an inn behind it." The man inside replies, "Ah Haa, in that case I expect also a little church to the right and we must be in Petersburgh." The man at the window says, "No, there isn't a church to the right, but there is a movie house." Whereupon the man inside says "Ah, in that case we are in North Walden." The point is that it takes collaboration between patient and therapist to formulate the best hypotheses about the meaning and nature of the patient's

38

symptoms and thoughts. (This process is really more helpful than free associating, which is only occasionally useful in brief therapy.)

Naturally, many patients are not capable of insight or cannot learn it fast enough to utilize it in brief intensive therapy. In that case, I ask the patient to give me concrete accounts of what he did in a particular instance, and ask him how he felt at different points. I will ask him about actual events that occurred prior to the therapeutic session, with regard to his family, work and other areas of his life. This gives me, and eventually the patient, some idea of what is going on in him, and is easier for him than real insightful reporting on his own, which requires psychological mindedness.

I will often ask very specific questions to elicit information as to what is going on in the patient: i.e., what he thought as he left the last session, what he had on his mind walking up the stairs on the way to the session. As noted earlier, I place particular emphasis on what might have been going on in someone's mind during the performance of *semi-automatic processes*, such as shaving, driving, making up, cooking; I usually learn a good deal from these thought processes. In addition, I usually ask the patient what he thought about just before he fell asleep, and upon awakening, and when rising from bed. And I *always* ask about dreams. If the patient tells me that he can't recall his dream, I always encourage him by asking whether he can at least recall a part of the dream, some feeling, or some word or picture, and thereupon the patient will very often report an entire dream, which usually produces very useful material to work with therapeutically.

3. Explaining the Therapeutic Process in Simplified Terms at the end of the Initial Session

In order to make the therapeutic process understandable to the patient, I will very often explain it in simplified terms at the end of the initial session or at some other occasion. My preferred conceptualization is to utilize the concept of apperceptive distortion (7). In essence, I explain to the patient that his past experience has been stored as a great number of images. When he views a contemporary scene, e.g., his foreman at work, he is likely to see him through a collage of past apperceptions of superior male figures such as his father, uncles, older brother, teacher, as though through a kaleidoscope. Neurotic or other pathological distortions are the result of an excessive influence of past apperceptions on contemporary cognition. The task of psychotherapy is to identify and understand the nature of the distortion of present cognition by past experiences and, in that way, bring about something akin to a perceptual correction and structural change.

4. Facilitating Learning

Above all, it has to be remembered that psychotherapy is a process of learning, unlearning, and relearning and that it is the therapist's task to facilitate this process by making it as concrete, as vivid, and as colorful as possible. I believe that nearly anything can be communicated to the patient, provided one finds the appropriate style for a given patient; even the "deepest" interpretation can be made after a relatively short time, provided it is done in the appropriate intellectual, conceptual and linguistic style.

In interpreting, it is very useful to use vivid examples to explain concepts. For instance, ambivalence can be humorously depicted as that mixed feeling one has when he sees his mother-in-law drive his brand new Cadillac off a cliff. I might illustrate self-harming behavior by the story of the man who stands in front of his burning house, laughing his head off. His neighbor comes over and says, "Joe, are you crazy? Your house is burning. What are you laughing for?" "Oh," says Joe, "That's all right. The bedbugs are finally getting it." To attempt to make some narcissistic behavior ego-alien for a start, I might relate the story of the poor bum who comes to see the wealthy man and tells him his hardluck story. He apparently succeeds in eliciting sympathy because tears roll down the multimillionaire's cheeks. The wealthy man reaches for the bell to summon his butler, and the bum's hopes soar. The butler arrives and the multimillionaire turns to him and demands, "Throw the bum out! He's breaking my heart!"

5. Projective Techniques

At times, as I said earlier, I find it useful to employ projective techniques as a vehicle for communication as well as interpretation. For example, using pictures from the Thematic Apperception Test or Rorschach blots one may get responses which indicate latent aggression. It may be possible for the therapist to point out to the patient that in every one of his responses, there is some form of aggression and, by that means, make the patient aware of his own excessive aggression. At times, it may be useful to point out that other people see quite different things in the picture than he did. In such a way, projective techniques may be used to increase the patient's psychological mindedness and make ego-alien what is often ego-syntonic for him.

6. The importance of education: In Emergency Treatment of Emotional Reaction to Physical Illness, Have Patient Sketch the Diseased Organ

Especially in the emergency treatment of emotional reactions to physical illness, it is useful to ask the patient to sketch the diseased organ. This often enables the therapist to observe a concrete illustration of the patient's distortions of reality. This approach also supplies an opportunity for informing the patient about the realities of his disorder, which are almost always easier to bear than the irrational notions and fantasies he has imagined.

It may be useful to conceptualize clearly the basic steps in brief intensive psychotherapy:

7. Communication Between the Patient and the Therapist

I have already discussed some ways of facilitating this process. Once the patient starts to communicate, the therapist starts to formulate some idea of common denominators between the patient's present behavior, past history, and the therapeutic relationship. When the therapist recognizes the common denominators and when the timing is correct, as determined by several technical criteria, the therapist should inform the patient of these common denominators.

8. Interpretation

The process of indicating the common denominators between the patient's behavioral and affective patterns in the past, present, and transference situations is generally known as interpretation. Clinically, interpretation may involve several preparatory steps and various forms of expression. A preparatory statement by the therapist might be to point up a behavior by saying, "This is remarkable." Sometimes, confronting the patient with a behavioral act is a form of interpretation, e.g., "Every time your sister is mentioned, you have kicked your leg." This is a form of interpretation saying "You seem to be angry at your sister." The confrontation, however, may have much more emotional impact. Some, like Davenloo (22), seem to use confrontation either primarily or exclusively, for which I see no reason: to the contrary, confrontation may be much too traumatic an intervention for some patients.

Although interpretation is *the* classical process of intervention in dynamic psychotherapy, it is, of course, by no means the only one, as will be discussed further on. However, again strictly schematically speaking, if the patient sees these common denominators, then the next step is insight.

9. Insight

If the patient is able to recognize the common denominators, he is applying insight. This is an "aha" experience, much like the expression of sudden awareness upon discovering a crossword puzzle answer or a jigsaw puzzle piece. The response must have strong affective components and not merely exist as an intellectual process.

10. Working Through

When the patient is able to apply his acquired insight to life situations, he is considered to be working through his problem. Working through can be defined as the application of insights learned in one situation to a variety of other situations: an insight with regard to a childhood situation may be applied to behavior in the transference situation and again in the contemporary work situation. This process may take place many times. What may start out as a

41

mostly conscious process of applying insights should increasingly become automatic and preconscious until ideally restructuring has taken place. This is basically a process of learning by conditioning, i.e., if the patient once again finds himself in a situation that might lead him to act out or feel panicky, he will instead apply his acquired insights. For additional details on the process of working through, see my paper on free association (4).

7.
METHODS OF INTERVENTION
in
INTENSIVE
BRIEF AND EMERGENCY PSYCHOTHERAPY
(B. E. P.)

METHODS OF INTERVENTION
in
B. E. P.

1. Interpretation

2. Catharsis and Mediate Catharsis

3. Auxiliary Reality Testing

4. Drive Repression

5. Sensitization to Signals

6. Education

7. Intellectualization

8. Support

9. Conjoint Sessions and Family Network Therapy

10. Psychoactive Drugs

METHODS OF INTERVENTION

While these methods are useful in psychoanalysis or any form of psycho-therapy, they are especially applicable in connection with the intensive process of brief therapy.

1. Interpretation

Interpretation is the classical method of intervention in dynamic psycho-therapy, but it is by no means the only one. (See Therapeutic Process.)

2. Catharsis and Mediate Catharsis

Catharsis can be an important intervention, although its role is exaggerated in such faddist therapies as primal scream. A common mistake is to believe that catharsis alone will have a therapeutic effect, when it is, by itself, rarely sufficient.

Mediate Catharsis is a term which I like to use when I express emotionally charged propositions for the patient. For example, with a depressed patient with a severe superego and a good deal of aggression, I may say, "Certainly if the foreman had done that to me, I would have kicked him." In this instance, I am expressing sentiments for the patient which might be too strong for his sensitive superego but, by virtue of my saying them, I take the superego responsibility for them. I hope that I also convey to the patient that if an authority such as I, the therapist, can permit himself such an aggressive thought, that it may not be so unacceptable. Identification and introjection of the therapist's image as a more benign part of the superego then plays an important role in this aspect of the therapeutic process.

Another form of indirect or mediate catharsis should be considered: "Of course, a conscientious person like yourself would not permit himself to think this, let alone to do it, but somebody else might certainly feel like killing the son-of-a-bitch." By this statement, the therapist gives the patient a double message: first, the reassurance that he would never lose such control and that, as a matter of fact, he is a person of strict conscience; and second, the idea that, in this instance, such aggressive sentiments are not inappropriate.

3. Auxiliary Reality Testing

Auxiliary reality testing is necessary in proportion to how distrubed a patient is and how great a need there is for the therapist to play the role of an auxiliary reality tester, clarifying the patient's distortions of reality and functioning as an auxiliary ego for him.

4. Drive Repression

Drive repression may be utilized with a patient who, in the instance of a woman, feels she ought to submit to peer pressure — e.g., with regard to promiscuity — but who has reacted or may predictably react to such behavior with panic. For example, in the case of an adolescent girl who feels that she has to engage in a certain amount of promiscuity to have social standing in her high school, I will flatly say that she simply should not engage in it. I will then help her to accept the idea that one does not have to be promiscuous to be accepted by one's peers. By this kind of directness, I hope to actually take a burden off her mind — or, at least, to arrange for a pause in which she can reconstitute. By selective inattention, one may sometimes discourage some forms of behavior and encourage others, in effect bringing about selective repression in the patient. It must be kept in mind, however, that repression has a normal role to play in daily functioning and that insufficient repression is, of course, at least as much a problem as is excessive repression.

5. Sensitization to Signals

Sensitization to signals is concerned with making the patient aware that certain behaviors on his part, whether acting out or panic, occur when there is a specific dynamic constellation. It may involve nothing more sophisticated than pointing out to a female patient that she always appears to have a flare-up with her husband in the two or three days preceding her period.

6. Education

Education of the above-mentioned patient might involve acquainting her with the facts about sodium retention and irritability and advising her to reduce her salt intake. The therapist might possibly prescribe a mild sedative for the two or three premenstrual days to help her avoid serious marital conflict.

7. Intellectualization

It has been mentioned that intellectualization plays a greater role in brief intensive therapy than in traditional longer-term therapies. It can be used in certain cases to increase the therapeutic alliance. In others — for example, with a very panicky patient — it helps to assure him that the therapist is at least intellectually understanding his symptom: Some control over what otherwise seems to the patient to be totally disruptive and ego-alien will come with such understanding.

8. Support

Support, in terms of the therapist's accepting feelings expressed by the patient — whether they be aggression, sexuality, or greed — makes it easier

46

for the patient to bear anxiety. Making reassuring statements is important at certain times in therapy, but it can never be the only measure taken if one expects to provide something more than just ad hoc help.

9. Conjoint Sessions and Family Network Therapy

Conjoint sessions and family network therapy (1) (41) are special techniques which cannot be dealt with in detail here, except to say that they can be used in brief intensive therapy in a very specific way. The therapist should clearly conceptualize what he wants to cover in a conjoint session and then arrange for that session to accomplish the circumscribed goals. The therapist's role is one of being a catalyst.

10. Psychoactive Drugs

My view of psychoactive drugs as a form of intervention is that they aid the therapist in the way anesthesia helps the surgeon: They provide a therapeutic field in which to work. In therapy, they are often part of the enabling conditions which make it possible to sufficiently control anxiety, disturbed thought processes or depression, so that it is possible for the patient to remain in the community and to continue with psychotherapy, which otherwise might be extremely difficult or impossible. Approach-anxiety will often keep a patient from facing certain insights. In such instances, anxiolytic drugs are useful in decreasing approach-anxiety, at least enough so that the patient is willing to deal with his problems in therapy. In patients with thought disorders, phenothiazines may greatly facilitate interaction in the short run or help to control impulses which may otherwise prove to be too disruptive. The main proposition concerning the usefulness of drugs in connection with psychotherapy is that one use enough medication to facilitate therapy but not so much as to interfere with motivation for further therapeutic work or cloud the cognitive processes to the point where it is impossible for the patient to participate in the psychotherapeutic process.

PART II

TEN MOST FREQUENT PSYCHIATRIC CONDITIONS AS PARADIGM

I
The Intensive
BRIEF AND EMERGENCY PSYCHOTHERAPY
(B. E. P.)
of
DEPRESSION

I. DEPRESSION

THEORETICAL CONSIDERATIONS

Depression is listed as the chief complaint by more than half of all people coming to outpatient clinics. That fact makes depression numerically significant, as well as important from a human standpoint. Also, the term depression is practically synonomous with misery: The possibility of suicide frequently exists, in which case treatment results are literally a matter of life and death. Prompt intervention — emergency psychotherapy — therefore plays a crucial role in the care and treatment of the depressed.

Depression is a broad term, certainly spanning different etiologies, as well as severities of the condition — a continuum ranging from mild reactive depressions to severe endogenous ones. Depressions may have biochemical, neurophysiological, as well as climatic and psychogenic pathogeneses, all of these interdependent. This chapter addresses itself only to nonpsychotic depressions. Nevertheless, I would like to say that I have found, in over 30 years of treating the depressed, that the same psychodynamic factors hold true for *most*, if not all, depressions, including endogenous ones. Systematic psychotherapeutic intervention can therefore be fairly generally formulated for most depressions. In many circumstances, emergency psychotherapy may be more promptly effective than antidepressant drugs, though it may be combined, of course, with drug treatment and, in fact, with any of the other modalities. Also, it should be noted that emergency psychotherapy of depressions may involve a dyadic relationship exclusively or consist of conjoint therapy and/or family therapy.

TEN SPECIFIC FACTORS IN THE PSYCHOTHERAPY OF DEPRESSION

1. PROBLEMS OF SELF-ESTEEM REGULATION

2. SEVERE SUPEREGO

3. (INTRA) AGGRESSION

4. LOSS

5. DISAPPOINTMENT

6. DECEPTION

7. STIMULUS HUNGER (ORALITY)

8. DEPENDENCE ON EXTERNAL NARCISSISTIC NUTRIENTS

9. DENIAL

10. DISTURBANCES IN OBJECT RELATIONS: THE DYADIC UNIT AND SYSTEMS THEORETICAL CONDITIONS

In the intensive Brief and Emergency psychotherapy of depression, the ten variables as stated above are the ones primarily to be addressed. The brief therapy of depression is distinguished, however, from long-term therapy or psychoanalysis of depression, by the emphasis on dealing with the first nine variables rather than the structural ones, which are the central ones in Jacobson's long-term therapy (31): namely, to restructure the patient's apperceptions, both self-representations and object representations, by the use of the transference relationship as interpolated introject (10). Some of these structural factors *may* be affected in brief therapy, but to expect any profound change would be too ambitious. These variables play a role in all depressions, and when addressed appropriately, have led to prompt therapeutic response in the vast majority of the patients I have been treating since I first described the rudiments of this technique in 1952 (3).

Though these are the main factors in *all* depressions, they play a role of *varying* importance in *each* depression. For instance, sometimes problems of insult to the self-esteem may play the primary role in precipitating the current depression. In other cases, a feeling of disappointment or deception may have triggered aggression, which, in the presence of a severe superego, leads to intra-aggression and not only depression but to potential suicidal danger.

In the brief psychotherapy of depression, it is important to listen for the presence and rank order of these factors in the individual patient, and to see the common denominators between the precipitating situation and historical circumstance. After listening to a careful history, I formulate a general treatment plan in terms of the general dynamics and structure of the condition and make an individual plan for the areas of intervention and methods of intervention suitable for the particular patient. As mentioned before (see Chapter 3), I may address myself in one patient to the loss of self-esteem and only after that turn to his aggression, intra-aggression, and severe superego. With another patient, I may primarily address myself to his severe superego and the intra-aggression and turn only later to orality and the feeling of deception and other factors. The methods of intervention may be any of those discussed before (see Chapter 7).

By vigorously working through the relevant factors with the appropriate methods of intervention, depression, in my experience, leads itself very well to brief intensive psychotherapy most of the time.

Following then are the treatment parameters which one can expect a psychotherapist to keep clearly in mind. This is not asking more of the psychotherapeutic intervention than one would of any medical or surgical intervention. One can expect that a surgeon approaching potential gall bladder surgery has a good grasp of the general propositions involved in the anatomy, physiology, and pathology of the gall bladder and its surrounding structures, and has a notion about the sequence of his interventions; he will modify the operation only as the individual circumstances demand.

52

1. Problems of Self-Esteem

Problems of self-esteem should be treated by:

a) Exploring the life history of the patient with regard to self-esteem or the lack of it (introjects, traumas, defects, level of aspiration).

b) Exploring recent insults to self-esteem.

c) Relating common denominators between past history and recent precipitating events for the purposes of interpretation, insight, and working through; discussing structural problems of self-esteem.

d) Taking pains to treat the patient with dignity.

e) Pointing out areas in a patient's life consonant with high self-esteem and reasons for it.

f) Dealing with aggression against the self, experienced by one part of the self against the other, and by examining the introjects and super-ego constituents and interpreting them, contrasting the historical origin with contemporary reality, and modifying them by the therapist's attitude.

g) Examining in detail the nature of ego ideals, the level of aspiration and the soundness of defenses, in an attempt to reduce the differential between unrealistic expectations and reality. Here the subdivisions of self-esteem promulgated by Bibring (20) are useful to keep in mind as a guide for specific therapeutic interventions.

h) Making any transference interpretations which seem especially suitable to this problem.

2. A Severe Superego

A severe superego should be treated by:

a) Understanding what components make it necessary to deflect aggression against the self. Treatment should include exploring the superego formation, its constituents, its manifestations, and the contemporary situation, finding common denominators between the past and the present, by interpretation, insight, and working through.

b) Using mediate catharsis, as I have described (see Chapter 7).

c) Inducing catharsis by encouraging the patient to express his feelings and pointing out their denial.

d) Examining any projections within the transference situation.

3. Intra-Aggression

The treatment of intra-aggression as a main variable should be pursued by:

a) Studying the life history and contemporary precipitating events for an understanding of who the primary object of the aggression might have been historically, and who it is currently. One has to relate the internalized objects against whom aggression was and is directed because of previous disappointment, deception, etc., to contemporary objects.

b) Making the patient aware of the fact that the contemporary objects who caused his current trauma, such as the love object or parental figure, have been apperceptively distorted by his experiences with the past one.

c) Making the patient aware that aggression may also be directed against self-representations, that is, one part of the self directs criticism against another part of the self.

Jacobson (31) suggested that it is part of the superego, formed to a large extent by internalization of parental figures, etc., which brings about guilt and depression. In distinction, she felt that one part of the self being critical of another part was the basic mechanism in depersonalization.

d) Dealing with the fact that self-esteem regulation plays such a major role in depression. It is clear that differences between the ego ideal — to be great, to be strong, to be clean — and the sense of self with regard to these goals, also plays an important role in intra-aggression.

4. A Feeling of Loss (of Love, of a Love Object, of Part of Oneself, of Possessions, of Self-Esteem)

A feeling of loss should be treated by:

a) Examining the life history particularly with regard to early losses, eliciting current precipitating events relating to a loss and helping the patient obtain insight by working through the current in relation to past traumas.

b) Examining the general nature of object relationships, the excessive dependent-passive demands which facilitate a feeling of disappointment.

c) Paying attention to the need for love, specifically in the transference situation.

5. Feelings of Disappointment

Depression primarily related to disappointment should be treated by:

a) Following Jacobson's concept of disappointment, the life history should be studied especially for previous events relating to the feeling of disappointment by love objects. Such disappointment may, of course, come about as innocently as through the loss of a loved figure by death, or the arrival of a sibling or, more chronically, by a lack of maternal responsivity. Depressed mothers easily provide disappointment for their offspring by virtue of their own unavailability.

b) Examining the precipitating event which triggered the depression for evidences of disappointment, and establishing common denominators between the earlier experiences of disappointment and contemporary feelings of this same nature, for the purposes of interpretation, insight, and working through. The transference relationship should be especially observed from this standpoint.

c) Dealing with the anger against the disappointing love object.

6. Feelings of Deception

A feeling of deception should be treated by:

a) Examining the life history for earlier episodes of deception. Deception used to be a customary part of the upbringing of children "because they were too small to know or understand the difference." One severely depressed young man had been left in Europe at age five by his parents with the promise that they would all be reunited soon. Actually, it took the parents two years to have the child rejoin them. The immediate precipitant for the depression which brought this patient into treatment was the fact that some "friends" of his used the occasion of a visit to set the stage for later robbing him.

b) Working through the paranoid features. People who have the feeling of having been deceived often present with more or less paranoid features and frequently have more difficulty in establishing lasting object relations than do other depressed patients. Therefore, the transference relationship will probably also be tenuous.

7. Orality and Stimulus Hunger

The treatment of orality and stimulus hunger as a main variable in depression should be pursued by:

a) Examining the patient's life history for evidences of the need for oral supplies and other stimuli, and the depressive reaction when they are not made available. This can be pointed out to the patient. In addition, common denominators will be readily found in the transference relationship.

b) Adopting a broad concept of oral needs. For this reason I prefer to use the term "stimulus hunger." This permits one to include the treatment of not only the classical oral needs, but also the need for love generally, and the need for input, sound, light, and human contact which is manifested in hypomanic situations and latent depressions. Depression is an organismic phenomenon of many subtypes, phenomenologically and etiologically. It is likely that some biochemical substratum, possibly genetically transmitted, is in two-way interaction with experiential factors. Both biochemical and experiential factors seem to relate to problems in the regulation of input and output of a broad spectrum of stimuli. Hypoactivity, neurologically and subjectively, may lead to stimulus hunger and, seemingly paradoxically, but clearly defensively, bring on the over-activity and excessive need for stimuli of the hypomanic and manic. Cyclic states constitute then different forms of coping with a physiological and psychological deficit.

c) Dealing, in this context, with Bertram Lewin's oral triad (36), the need to devour, the wish to be devoured, and the wish to sleep.

8. Narcissism

Depressed patients usually have more secondary narcissism than (other) neurotic patients. Their object relations are usually primarily of an anaclitic nature. Their narcissistic needs are closely related to the orality and stimulus hunger discussed above. One can, in fact, speak of their need for *narcissistic nutrients*. Their narcissism, however, is also specifically related to their patho-logical forms of self-esteem regulation.

As a main variable in depression, narcissism should be treated by:

a) Examining the patient's attempts to regulate intake of stimuli of all kinds. In this instance, a depressed person may be compared to a poikilotherm animal in distinction to the non-depressive, which may be compared to the homoiotherm. People who attain a warm inter-nalized love object can be remarkably independent of external supplies, and not become significantly depressed even after rather depressing experiences. Like the homoiotherm's body temperature, their self-esteem temperature is well buffered. People who were not that fortunate are more like poikilotherms (popularly misnamed cold-blooded animals because if exposed to low external temperature, their body temperature goes down.) Similarly, if the depressed have chilling emotional experiences, their self-esteem decreases catastrophically, and their need for external narcissistic nutrients increases sharply.

The depressive personality is easily depressed when there is not enough stimulus input of such factors as self-esteem, a feeling of being loved especially, and other stimuli. In his attempt to regulate this stimulus hunger, the depressed patient often has to walk a difficult line between overstimulation and understimulation, between being overreactive and tense or being hypoactive and depressed.

b) Giving special attention to the education and planning of the patient's life. Such a person must learn to recognize the signals for disappointment and depletion, and guard against let-down after very gratifying experiences. It would be a serious mistake for such an individual to enter a career such as show business, where one's whole life is dependent on mercurial changes in narcissistic nutrients.

c) Attending to the excessive need to be loved and to have other narcissistic gratifications, because of the lack of health in the form of good introjects. It is the resulting feeling of emptiness which is often perceived as coming from the outside, and is related to the previously discussed need for input, feelings of low self-esteem, poor object relationships, and taking the self as one's own love object. This is discussed in detail by Jacobson (31).

d) Taking into account that the stimulus hunger as well as the liability with regard to narcissism are most likely related to a biochemical disturbance.

9. Denial

The treatment of denial as the major defense mechanism in depression should be addressed by:

a) Examining the life history for previous occurrences of denial and whether they were followed by subsequent depressions or elations.

b) Establishing continuity where there is discontinuity may point out the denied affect. This alone will frequently rapidly reverse a depression. Denial as the outstanding defense mechanism in affective disorders (especially the hypomanic state) was most extensively discussed by Bertram Lewin (36). He described the thought processes involved in it as centrifugal. This process can indeed be most interestingly observed in truly manic patients, especially if one tries to have them face their denied affect. In depressed patients, the traumatic event, namely the disappointment, deception, or enraging event is often denied. I suspect that this is so in the case of many depressions which are considered endogenous by nondynamic psychiatrists, simply because the precipitating event was denied by the patient and not clearly evident in the life history as obtained by the dynamically uninformed. This is, of course, different in clearly reactive depressions, where only the relationship to the internalized object is denied.

c) Using both mediate catharsis, as previously described, and also direct catharsis. Limited as the use of ventilation is (9), it is very helpful in the lifting of depression after the cathartic interpretation of the denied affect and the denied events. It is important that one help the patient to express his rage at the person precipitating the current depression, as well as against the related introjects.

10. Object Relations

Disturbances in object relations, as a main variable in depression, should be treated by:

a) Examining the life history for the nature of object relations. In the depressed, object relations are often of an anaclitic nature, with oral clinging playing a predominant role. The narcissism and the need for narcissistic supplies has already been pointed out, as well as orality in a broad sense. In the history of the depressed, oral deprivation, or especially a mixture of overindulgence and deprivation, plays an important role.

Critical parents are often the cause of an excessive level of aspiration, and the correspondingly low self-esteem. The need to please others, with the nearly build-in conditions for failing, play a marked role.

In the seriously depressed, symbiotic relationships with the concomitant difficulties in self-boundaries, are prevalent.

b) Constantly referring to the transference relationship in the brief intensive therapy. From the start, one has to warn the patient that he may be too easily disappointed and want to break off treatment. From the first session on, one has to help the patient anticipate and work through the separation and disappointment and the rage which might ensue and threaten the therapeutic result.

c) Ending brief and emergency psychotherapy on a positive transference note is of prime importance. It is unlikely that one can indeed affect the structural problems pertaining to object relationships for permanent change. But one can and must deal with the dynamic problems for prompt therapeutic effect.

d) Keeping in mind the dyadic unit and systems theoretical considerations. Very often I have been struck with the fact that the depressed person alternates in mood, from a normal mood to a depression, as part of an *interaction with another significant person*. For instance, one woman frequently suffered from depression because her husband made excessive demands on her, enraged her and denigrated her. Her first responses, over several weeks, were always compliance and she was, in essence, putting herself in the position of a Geisha girl. After a time, she would become depressed and unable to perform any household chores or other tasks which the husband found for her. At that point her husband would become very solicitous. After I helped her out of the depression, she would become slightly elated and somewhat assertive and would engage in shopping sprees and a good deal of social activity. In due course, the husband would become severely critical of her. She should thereupon enter her Geisha cycle and later become depressed.

In this type of depression, it rarely sufficies to treat only the identified patient. It is important to include the significant other in treatment and that may sometimes, though not necessarily, take the therapeutic situation out of the brief therapy range. In other instances of depression, the identified patient is part of a more complex system, sometimes familial, sometimes in relation to work, with similar interactions.

II.

The Intensive
BRIEF AND EMERGENCY PSYCHOTHERAPY
(B.E.P.)
of
ACTING OUT

II. ACTING OUT

CONCEPTUAL CONSIDERATIONS

The term "acting out" is widely used, often loosely employed, but the phenomenon is of great clinical importance.

Looking for established definitions of "acting out", we find that English and English (23) have defined acting out briefly as *manifesting the purposive behavior appropriate to an older situation in a new situation which symbolically represents it.* Hinsie and Campbell (30) have defined it as *the partical discharge of instinctual tension that is achieved by responding to the present situation as if it were the situation that originally gave rise to the instinctual demand.* Whereas both definitions are useful, neither fully encompasses the scope of this phenomenon. The narrowest definition of acting out is one reserved for patients in classical analysis referring to behavior related to the transference neurosis: In essence, the patient makes a statement in the form of inappropriate action instead of appropriate verbalization. The loosest use of the term equates it virtually with action, and thus makes it useless.*

The range of phenomena usefully included in the concept of acting out sometimes characterizes brief acts of circumscribed and merely episodic nature; e.g., an obese person is sometimes said to be acting out his sense of frustration and his need for gratification by overeating. Of course, the dynamics may be much more complex, but the essential implication here is that such a person, feeling frustrated, disappointed, and unloved, translates these usually unconscious feelings into the act of feeding himself. The act of eating symbolically represents the unstated verbalization, "Nobody loves me, nobody feeds me. Therefore, I have to feed myself," or "I feel empty, I feel deflated. I wish to have the feeling of being full and solid." It is obvious that drinking may have the same unverbalized meaning. One may say, in such instances, that *the term acting out is used when certain behaviour seems to make a simple unconscious statement.* It is this quality of making an unconscious statement that differentiates acting out from other neurotic behavior with phobic or obsessive activity, as well as the fact that acting out is usually ego-syntonic, at least at the moment of action. (Overeating, however, as a simple form of acting out, is often ego-alien and may be perceived as compulsive by sophisticated people.)

---

* For a detailed discussion of this topic, see *The Concept of Acting Out: Theoretical Considerations* (6).

Another conceptually simple use of the term acting out is frequently encountered in discussions of psychotic behavior. An assaultive attack may be considered as the acting out of delusional and hallucinatory distortions: the behavior is consistent with and caused by the distortions, and has little or nothing to do with reality. When we ask ourselves, in dealing with psychotics, "Is this patient likely to act out?" we are wondering what the chances are that he will act upon his unrealistic perceptions and impulses. The question is one that has enormous therapeutic and social import, and it is an urgent task that we understand and develop reliable criteria why certain individuals are able to sustain indefinitely paranoid feelings and vicious notions without ever doing harm, and others are sometimes pressed and overrun by similar impulses into the performance of dreadfully destructive acts. Fortunately, only a small percentage of psychotics translate their distorted perceptions into action.

Another rather simple form of acting out is also characteristic of the hysterical personality. What impresses one most strongly about such individuals is the tremendous mood swings, from love to hate, from depression to elation, with actions correspondingly extremely different, appearing at rather short time intervals.

For clinical purposes, the most useful conception of acting out is probably that a patient expresses a thought or feeling in action rather than by verbalization, when the latter would be the cultural norm. This definition leaves one to determine, in each case, why the impulse was acted upon — for genetic, transferential, neurological (as in ADD) or other reasons. If I would have to choose the most frequent cause for acting out, which brings people to emergency psychotherapy, it would probably be reactive to acutely lowered self-esteem, such as the loss of love, of a job, etc., which threatens to lead to violence against the self or others.

The ensuing interventions have primarily this type of situation in mind.**

** For Acting Out specifically referring to behavior in the therapeutic situation, see *Crises and Special Problems in Psychoanalysis and Psychotherapy* (12).

TEN SPECIFIC FACTORS IN THE THERAPEUTIC MANAGEMENT OF ACTING OUT

1. BARGAIN FOR A DELAY

2. MAKE THE ACT EGO-ALIEN

3. MAKE A "CATHARTIC" INTERPRETATION OF THE UNDERLYING DRIVE

4. INCREASE SIGNAL AWARENESS AND SENSITIZE PATIENT TO CUES

5. PREDICT WHEN PATIENT WILL ACT OUT

6. STRENGTHEN THE SUPEREGO

7. REMOVE THE PATIENT FROM A PROVOCATIVE SETTING

8. ENLIST THE HELP OF OTHERS

9. DRUGS

10. BRIEF HOSPITALIZATION

1. Bargain for a Delay

A critical factor in the therapeutic management of acting out is to bargain for a delay. People who act out characteristically seek immediate impulse discharge. Much of their pleasure lies in the immediacy of the acting out, and, therefore, any delay is likely to mitigate much of the temptation. Most typically, I ran across this problem as consultant to a suicide prevention clinic. Somebody would call up on the hot line and say, "I'm sitting on a window-sill and I am about to jump out the window." My suggestion to the social worker was to say, "Look, there's nothing I can do about it if you want to jump. Nobody can prevent you. On the other hand, nobody can prevent you from doing it tomorrow either so I suggest that you postpone it a bit and come in and we can discuss it. Then, if you still feel like it, that's your decision." By such means, one may not only attain the crucial delay, but also the chance to intervene. But often the delay alone is sufficient to remove the main danger. Part of the gratification in acting out is the patient's feeling of omnipotence; if one can interfere with that, as by arranging a delay, one has achieved an important goal.

2. Make the Act Ego-Alien

The thereapist must also try to make the act ego-alien. If the therapist understands the historical components behind the acting out, he can specify to the patient the common denominators between the current acting out and his previous life history. I thus suggest to the patient that, in essence, he is being computer programmed by his past and that instead of acting out on his own volition, he is instead being motivated to act by unconscious factors. By this technique, I try to make ego-alien what seems ego-syntonic and that spoils much of the fun, including the feeling of omnipotence.

3. Make a "Cathartic" Interpretation of the Underlying Drive

Another important intervention is to make a cathartic interpretation of the underlying drive. A cathartic interpretation, as pointed out elsewhere (19), is one that interprets unconscious material long before it is preconsciously available to the patient, in the hope of cutting through several layers and decreasing the push from the unconscious material. One might, in that case, interpret the meaning of a certain kind of acting out, translating it freely; e.g., "You want to do that because it makes you feel big and you felt so small when XYZ happened."

4. Increase Signal Awareness and Sensitize Patient to Cues

It is important to sensitize the patient to cues that are likely to set him off. It is helpful, for example, to try to predict when people who habitually act out will do so again so that it can be discouraged. The circumstances (i.e., the setting and the dynamic constellation) in which the patient will act out should be determined. A banal but important example relates to habitual quarreling and violence precipitated by premenstrual tension. Because many women react with water retention and irritability only to ovulation in one ovary, they are often not aware of the regularity with which premenstrual tension leads to aggression and domestic quarreling. I point out to them that it occurs every other month, premenstrually, and attempt to explain the mechanism of water-retention and irritability, potassium and sodium metabolism, and other bodily changes. I often suggest that as soon as they note a minimal flow, tenderness in the breast, or water retention or irritability, that they guard themselves especially against violent outbursts, possibly taking a tension reducing drug for the two or three days prior to menstruation.

5. Predict When Patient Will Act Out

One of the most effective ways to deal with acting out is to systematically and intentionally predict for the patient under what circumstances he is likely to act out. By getting the specific details of events surrounding the acting-out, the therapist can usually find clues as to what precipitates the process of acting out and can clearly predict that the patient will behave the same way again when he encounters the same situation. The therapist, of course, couches this *in hopes that his prediction will turn out to be wrong*. This increases signal awareness of cues that are likely to forewarn acting out, and such awareness, combined with making the behavior ego-alien, will obviate the need for acting out.

6. Strengthen the Superego

Under certain circumstances, it may be important to strengthen the superego. One may have to explain the destructive consequences to others of certain kinds of acting out and appeal to the patient's conscience. With a suicidal patient, one might point out that taking her own life will not only severely damage her younger child but will also be devastating to her husband and parents.

7. Remove the Patient From a Provocative Setting

If somebody is in a life situation that is likely to precipitate acting out, such as a pathogenic family situation or a work situation that encourages a paranoid reaction, it is essential to remove the patient from that unhealthy setting.

A clinical example is that of a male patient in early adolescence who is sleeping with his mother. This is bound to lead to acting out on his part, be it homosexual, heterosexual, or violent behavior. It will be impossible to deal with the patient's problem as long as he continues to sleep with his mother. In many cases, the patient lives in a situation which chronically provides over-stimulation. The acting out under these circumstances is an attempt to "blow off steam." The therapist acts as the patient's auxiliary reality tester, pointing out what triggers the acting out, and takes a very positive role in changing the setting.

8. Enlist the Help of Others

It may be essential to enlist the help of others in the patient's life to prevent the acting out, even in relatively simple situations. I once treated a college student with a marked success neurosis who was going to fail to graduate because he was simply frightened of taking his examinations. Neither interpretation nor drug treatment enabled him to cope with this crippling anxiety, which was a form of acting out his success neurosis. I therefore engaged the help of his fiancee and asked her to walk him to the examination room. This she did, but we soon discovered that as soon as she left the room he would also leave, sometimes by another door. I finally had to ask her to sit right next to him while he was taking his exams. By such means, he managed to graduate, and his particular problems were dealt with subsequently.

9. Drugs

At times, it may be helpful to use drugs in treatment. Anxiolytic drugs are, of course, essential in decreasing approach-anxiety, phenothiazines are helpful in treating psychotic thought disorders, and methylphenidate, tricyclics and other drugs often have a controlling effect on people with ADD. If a patient is experiencing premenstrual tension or a migraine headache with visual symptoms, dizziness, nausea, etc., the use of a drug like diphenylhydantoin is indicated and may help avoid explosive acting-out.

10. Brief Hospitalization

If nothing else is likely to prove effective, the patient should be hospitalized temporarily to get him over the most critical phase of his condition.

III

The Intensive
BRIEF AND EMERGENCY PSYCHOTHERAPY
(B.E.P.)
of
SUICIDE

III. SUICIDE

THEORETICAL CONSIDERATIONS

To understand and treat suicidal threats in brief intensive therapy, one should keep in mind the points discussed in the treatment of depression and the therapy of acting out. After all, most, although by no means all, suicidal people are depressed, and suicide frequently shares many of the characteristics of acting out. Acutely suicidal people, those whom Shneidman (52) considers to have high lethality and high perturbation, require special treatment measures, as discussed later. In Shneidman's scheme, what he calls lethality, the acute suicidalness, is of limited duration. Unless one can "do it" then and there, it's no "fun". Along with acting out, the impulse or urge to commit suicide is often associated with a need for immediacy.

Depressed people are not necessarily the only ones or even the most likely ones to be serious suicidal dangers. Panic often plays the primary role. For instance, former U. S. Defense Secretary Forrestal, in a panic, thought that the Russians were after him and jumped out of a window to escape them. One patient had the delusional and hallucinatory fear of being caught in a net and stabbed while helplessly entangled. Suicide seemed a reasonable way out of such torture. One young man had torturously nagging, obsessive and delusional symptoms, and finally, in a desperate attempt to end them, threw himself down a stairwell. Another patient had "command" hallucinations urging him to jump out of a window. Such voices are almost invariably the voices of the superego, and people suffering from such hallucinations are first-rank suicide risks.

Schizophrenic patients can be in a variety of panics, such as those of a paranoid or homosexual nature. Or they may suffer from the terror of the awareness of disintegration. The cognitive changes that accompany their illness may so frighten them that they will attempt suicide. These kinds of panics are often more lethal than depression. In some severely dissociated patients, one might see what looks like "depression," but might be more properly called desperation. One man who was diagnosed as schizophrenic suffered mainly from minimal brain dysfunction, and was desperate about his inability to control his impulses. It took all his energy to maintain control, such that he could scarcely perform any work. He was a bright young man whose struggles were heartbreaking to see. This individual was a serious suicide risk.

An additional and often curious factor which should be kept in mind when assessing suicidal risk is the individual's *concept of death*. Surprisingly, these concepts vary greatly. Many people, primarily those with a great deal of orality, seem to have the idea that death is a form of sleep, some sort of refreshing repose from which they will awaken with all their problems having been resolved. When attempting suicide, such people will most often ingest toxins, in keeping with their oral organization. In our culture, these agents will most often be sleeping pills. This suicidal risk group would include a large number of depressed people, quite in accordance with Lewin's concept of the oral tried, namely the wish to sleep, to devour, and to be devoured.

The availability of instruments for suicide, as well as cultural factors, plays a role in the particular method chosen. For instance, the oral route is most likely to be the one chosen by women, while more men than women use guns and knives. Gas used in cooking or fumes from an automobile are methods frequently chosen in this culture, since seemingly painless means are preferred. Most people don't relish the thought of hurting themselves badly, in the sense of inflicting physical pain, even though they may not mind killing themselves. An odd extension of this wish to avoid self-harm while annihilating oneself is the old coroner's rule that if the bullet passed through the jacket, it was probably murder, not suicide. Ironically, not wishing to damage valuable clothing is in this sense actually denying the life-destroying nature of the act. Most suicides would first take off the jacket and carefully fold it, or at least push it aside.

Some people actually fantasize themselves surving the suicide and standing at their graveside laughing happily at all those people who are sorry that they weren't nicer to the deceased.

In the initial session anamnesis, there are two specific factors which are crucial to keep in mind.

1. A Family History With Regard to Suicide

It has seemed to me at times that there may be a familial tendency to commit suicide, not necessarily even related to very severe depression. Since this tendency may virtually appear as an independent variable, any patient with a family history of suicide should be considered a greater risk than the immediate clinical situation per se warrants.

2. Other Acts of Violent Acting Out

This second factor in personal history is also crucial. In my experience, this has seemed to hold true especially for people with a history of having killed household pets, either as children or as adults: It has seemed to me that having been "able" to express such unbridled impulses is consistent with violent self-harm.

TEN SPECIFIC FACTORS IN THE
THERAPEUTIC MANAGEMENT
of
SUICIDAL PATIENTS

1. PRECIPITATING FACTOR OR SITUATION
   (DEPRESSION OR PANIC)

2. CONTENT AND CONCRETENESS AND PRIMITIVITY OF
   FANTASIES AND PLANS

3. PREVIOUS ATTEMPTS (OR PLANS) AND ATTENDING
   CIRCUMSTANCES

4. FAMILY HISTORY OF SUICIDALITY AND/OR
   DEPRESSION

5. IF ACUTELY SUICIDAL: ABANDON THERAPEUTIC
   NEUTRALITY, ETC.

6. WORK WITH TUNNEL VISION

7. BARGAIN FOR A DELAY AND USE OTHER VARIABLES
   INVOLVED IN ACTING OUT

8. WORK WITH FACTORS PERTAINING TO *DEPRESSION
   OR PANIC*

9. DRAW SIGNIFICANT OTHERS INTO THE SITUATION:
   COMMUNITY RESOURCES

10. DRUGS, HOSPITALIZATION

1. Precipitating Factor or Situation

Most frequently, suicidalness is related to depression. However, as mentioned previously, some of the most vicious suicide attempts are also made in panics, especially psychotic panics. All the precipitating factors discussed under depression (see Part II, Ch. I) and panic (see Part II, Ch. IX) and acting out (Part II, Ch. II) are relevant here.

Note: It is not easy to differentiate the psychodynamics of suicide from those we understand to be involved in all depressions. The expression of the wish to die is most often an oral wish to sleep without cares, as Lewin has pointed out (36). Oral wishes such as these are widespread and are probably responsible for the frequency of suicidal thoughts in the general population, especially among adolescents. When such oral wishes, however, are accompanied by a great deal of hostility in people with little ego strength and with a severe superego, the therapist has much to be concerned about. Understanding the specific dynamics of the suicidal impulse becomes important. Among those which may be operating are: the wish to expiate a real or imagined crime; a desire for revenge; the wish for reunion with a deceased mate or lover; the desire to force love from other people. Thus, the motivations that may result in a suicidal act do not always follow the same pattern, although the element of depression is common to most of them.

2. Content and Concreteness and Primitivity of Fantasies and Plans

If there is any reason to suspect suicidal notions or fantasies, it is essential that the therapist insist that the patient spell them out, in as much concrete detail as possible. The explicit statement of all suicidal notions may have a cathartic effect and facilitate reality testing by both patient and therapist. Any unrealistic notions about death should be clarified, for example, the fantasy that one will really survive suicide and wake up as if from a sleep.

Either from the conscious fantasy or from any other material, the therapist must discover against whom the aggression is unconsciously intended. Analytically speaking, it is essential to understand which introject the aggression is meant for; i.e., one must understand to which *earlier introject* the *contemporary figure* who provides the disappointment, deception, or other insult is related. In this context, transference sentiments, i.e., hostility toward the therapist, are frequently responsible for suicidal ideas, and should be identified and interpreted.

The more primitive the fantasies are, the greater the risk of suicide. People who can contemplate self-mutilation, e.g., gauging out one's eyes, disemboweling oneself, slitting one's throat, show alarming lack of impulse control. Cultural factors, as always, have to be taken into consideration, but, in general, the relative primitivity of fantasy correlates to the primitivity of personality structure and to severity of problems of impulse control.

71

3. Previous Attempts and Plans

The most important criterion for the likelihood of suicide is a previous serious attempt. Shneidman and Farberow (53) have noted that most successful suicide victims had attempted or threatened suicide previously. Serious attempts are those in which the patient had a high probability of dying and was discovered by an unpredictable coincidence, or where he managed to survive a truly life-threatening situation. These cases stand out in distinction to someone who took a few pills or slashed his or her wrists superficially. Such attempts are usually more in the nature of a gesture, but also should not be disregarded. In general, as mentioned, the *more concretely someone plans suicide*, e. g., leaving detailed instructions about a will, having a specific scenario in terms of method, time, place, etc., *the greater the risk*. Shneidman (51), who has made a study of suicide notes, underscores the portentiousness of concreteness. The more concrete the plans that someone has made for committing suicide, the more cause for concern. However, absence of plans is no reason for ignoring suicidal tendencies; some patients who attempt suicide only as a gesture may "accidentally" overdo it and succeed only too well.

4. Family History of Suicidality and/or Depression

As mentioned previously, a family history of suicide and/or a history of violent acting out in other forms, especially in childhood, is ominous. People who killed pets or injured playmates as children are prime risks. This stands to reason dynamically, since intra-aggression and aggression against others often seem to be correlated, the common denominator being a high level of aggression and poor impulse control. An example which illustrates this is that of Goebbels, the Nazi criminal, who was personally responsible for the torture and death of thousands. In defeat, he killed his wife and children, and then committed suicide.

5. If Acutely Suicidal, Abandon Therapeutic Neutrality

If the patient is extremely suicidal, and has what Shneidman would call "high lethality," *one has to abandon therapeutic neutrality*. It is necessary to be supportive, reassure the patient, make him realize that there are other choices available besides the one of self-destruction, and assure him that one will be available around the clock. With the patient's permission, if possible, family members should be informed of the situation. The therapist should acquaint the patient with the availability of crisis lines and services in the community, just in case the therapist himself is not accessible.

6. Work With Tunnel Vision

Suicidal patients suffer from "tunnel vision" and only see one particular solution. It is therefore important to show them that there are other options (see Shneidman's case study of a highly suicidal patient, as an excellent example of lowering lethality by working with tunnel vision [52]).

7. Bargain for a Delay and Use Other Variables Involved in Acting Out

See Chapter on Acting Out

8. Work with Factors Pertaining to Depression or Panic

See Chapters on Depression and Panic

9. Draw Significant Others Into the Situation: Community Resources

If there is a serious concern about the possibility of suicide, one should not hesitate to take appropriate measures. Attempting to carry all the responsibility oneself is likely to produce considerable anxiety and the communication of that anxiety may only alarm the patient and make him more suicidal. If the therapist has an acute enough concern, it may be useful, with the patient's agreement or, if necessary, without it, to call a relative to the office and arrange for him to accompany the patient home. It may even be necessary to temporarily abandon therapeutic neutrality and take the patient home or to a hospital oneself.

Shneidman suggests that, since suicide is often a "highly charged dyadic crisis," the therapist consider working with the significant other in the patient's life, be it parent, spouse, or homosexual lover (52). It is not suggested that the significant other be seen as often as the patient, but that they be directly involved.

Community resources should also be relied upon, especially hot lines and other emergency centers.

Family and social networks (e. g., friends and peers in the case of adolescents or college students), as well as brief group therapy to supplement the dyadic relationship, may be desirable.

10. Drugs, Hospitalization

It is very useful for the therapist to know who the patient's internist or general practitioner is and establish some liaison, just in case an acute suicidal attempt is made. In this event, the medical person will be much better equipped than the therapist to deal with the life-threatening emergency. Generally, it is very useful for anybody engaged in the treatment of relatively severely disturbed people to have a close working relationship with a hospital so that the patient can be briefly hospitalized, if necessary, to tide him over a particular danger. Active working-through can be done in that protective setting. Of course, pharmacotherapy and, in very rare instances, ECT, may be indicated.

Coda: In dealing with suicidal patients, one has to remember that there are still many variables that we don't fully understand. As in any serious condition, one has to accept some losses. One young man, on the threshold of a promising medical career, killed himself in a hotel room with an overdose of sleeping pills. The suicide note he left had been written ten years previously! No one who worked with him or knew him personally at the time of his death had discerned any change in his behavior or was aware of any circumstances that might have precipitated his tragic death at the particular time it occurred.

IV.
ENABLING CONDITIONS FOR
THE AMBULATORY B.E.P.
of
PSYCHOTICS

IV. ENABLING CONDITIONS FOR THE AMBULATORY BRIEF AND EMERGENCY PSYCHOTHERAPY OF PSYCHOTICS

THEORETICAL CONSIDERATIONS

The intensive brief and emergency psychotherapy of acutely disturbed psychotics can be one of the most rewarding of therapeutic experiences. It is frequently possible to effect a dramatic loss of symptoms and general improvement of the acute manifestations of the disorder rather promptly. It often enough holds true that after the acute phase has been successfully dealt with, there remain the characterological features which are of complex nature and that often require prolonged and patient treatment. The present discussion, however, addresses itself only to the circumstances necessary for the treatment of the acute phase of a psychotic episode.

Certainly the first question that must arise in the treatment of an acutely disturbed psychotic on an ambulatory basis, in the private office, social agency, or a clinic, must be whether a patient is suitable for this type of treatment.

Therefore, I want to address myself to the necessary conditions, the conditions that enable one to perform intensive brief and emergency ambulatory psychotherapy with acute psychotics. If the enabling conditions outlined cannot be met, ambulatory psychotherapy may not be advisable, and an alternate mode of treatment may be indicated.

TEN ENABLING CONDITIONS FOR THE INTENSIVE BRIEF AND EMERGENCY PSYCHOTHERAPY OF PSYCHOTICS

1. A REASONABLY COOPERATIVE, NON-ASSAULTIVE PATIENT: FACILITATING COMMUNICATION

2. AT LEAST ONE STABLE RELATIONSHIP IN THE PATIENT'S LIFE

3. A CLOSE RELATIONSHIP WITH A NEARBY HOSPITAL

4. OPTIMALLY, A FAMILY NETWORK

5. AVAILABILITY OF AN AUXILIARY THERAPIST

6. AWARENESS OF FAMILY AND COMMUNITY RESOURCES: THE "Y"' OVR, ETC.

7. HOT LINES AND EMERGENCY CENTERS

8. ACCESS TO AN ALARM SYSTEM: DO NOT BE A HERO!

9. A SUITABLE HOUSING SITUATION

10. DRUG THERAPY IN COMBINATION WITH PSYCHOTHERAPY

1. A Reasonably Cooperative, Non-Assaultive Patient: Facilitating Communication

One of the most obvious enabling conditions is that one has to have *a reasonably cooperative, non-assaultive patient*. By reasonably cooperative, I mean that he at least comes to the session or is willing to be brought by a third party. However, it may be possible to start B. E. P. with a patient who is unwilling to come to therapy. Sometimes it is necessary to visit the patient in his own home, at least to initiate therapy. When this is not possible or feasible, an effective means of getting an unwilling patient to the office is to instruct a family member to ask the patient to accompany him to see the psychotherapist for his — the relative's — own sake. It is usually true enough that the relative is deeply concerned and upset, and is being sincere when he tells the patient that he wants some help for dealing with some of his own problems. Often the patient is then willing to come along as a mute companion. The initial exchanges are all between the therapist and the patient's relative. It must be part of the therapist's skill to eventually engage the patient until he or she slowly becomes the main interactor and ultimately the sole one.

One other possibility of engaging a patient in treatment, if the above procedure is ineffectual, is to engage in *mediate interpretations*. If a patient refuses to come by himself or even with a companion, as described above, it may be possible to learn enough about the psychodynamics of the patient from the relative to suggest statements or interpretations which the relative can then relay back to the patient. If, in turn, the relative reports back to the therapist, he can be used to mediate the therapy in such a way that the patient might be affected beneficially enough to a point where he is willing to come for treatment with the relative as companion. Then the therapist can proceed as above.

The fact that many psychotics may start out mute or barely communicative is no contraindication to therapy. Even potential assaultiveness need not be a contraindication, provided one sets up certain conditions which I will discuss later, with regard to certain precautions and the possible concomitant use of drugs. Of course, I include patients in ambulatory psychotherapy who are often actively deluded and hallucinated. Most of us are aware of the fact that in many patients extensive delusions and hallucinations need not necessarily interfere with seemingly normal social behavior. There is many a patient who thinks he is Jesus Christ or believes he can understand what the birds are saying, but nevertheless may continue to hold a skilled job and arrive punctually for each of his appointments. Although some patients may not be well enough to come on their own by car or bus, they may still profit from ambulatory psychotherapy, if someone brings them to the therapist's office.

The premise is that, whenever possible, it is better to avoid hospitalization, provided the patient is not actively homicidal or suicidal or so disturbed as to do harm inadvertently. The fact is that very little competent psychotherapy is offered in any hospital. In university-affiliated institutions, residents are usually the ones directly treating the patient, even though under supervision. Though they may be competent, the fact is they are still at an early stage of their training. In private institutions, there are usually not enough psychotherapists available, or else the therapists available are of questionable competence. The cost of hospitalization often approaches $100,000 a year. In addition, regression and secondary gain from being cared for ("nursed") produce other problems. Very frequently, the patient's reentry into the community, if it is not extremely skillfully handled, starts a new flare-up.

2. One Stable Relationship in the Patient's Life

Less obvious and less generally considered is the almost absolute need for at least *one stable relationship in the patient's life situation* — at least one person, such as parent, spouse, child, close friend — anybody whom one might turn to if the circumstances should warrant it. The therapist must be able to talk to somebody who is willing to keep an eye on the patient at home, because of concerns about suicide, or other potentially harmful situations; someone who can take a helpful role if the patient should require hospitalization, or can otherwise serve as a constructive influence in the patient's life. Without at least a single stable person close to the patient, I have found through bitter experience that one may be left with almost impossible situations, more responsibility than one can reasonably handle, and with less safety than is essential for the treatment situation.

3. A Close Relationship With a Nearby Hospital

The third enabling condition for anybody who wants to treat rather acutely disturbed psychotics is that one have a *close relationship with a nearby hospital*, including a general hospital willing to take psychiatric patients. It is essential in treating acute psychotics that one be willing to take reasonable risks. Those reasonable risks include the possibility that some patients will become disturbed in the course of treatment, either for adventitious reasons or for reasons intrinsic to the treatment. The therapist can engage in psychotherapy with acutely disturbed people only if he feels safe enough. He needs an arrangement which permits almost instant hospitalization of the patient, should the need arise. At times, even only two or three days of hospitalization can make a crucial difference. This provision certainly helps to give one more therapeutic freedom with less anxiety for patient and therapist. The hospital provides some immediate protection for the patient and gives the therapist freedom to engage in interventions which might possibly be usetting to the patient.

Though therapeutic freedom sometimes has to include interventions which might prove unnerving to the patient, I do not believe in inducing regressions intentionally: I am not certain that therapeutically induced regressions and dissociations may not lay the foundation for easier regression and dissociation at other times, and therefore do not consider them a desirable therapeutic modality.

However, I do believe in the value of such active steps as cathartic interpretations, i. e., interpreting unconscious material directly a la John Rosen (47), without waiting until it becomes preconscious, as is more customary in the treatment of less disturbed people.

Aside from the importance of having easy access to a hospital, it is extremely desirable that it be a hospital setting in which one can continue to see and treat one's own patient while he is there. This type of situation is often difficult to attain because teaching hospitals always insist on having only their residents and staff treat patients. In view of this fact, proprietary hospitals, which may be otherwise less desirable, are to be preferred. While the patient is hospitalized for an acute disorder, actively deluded and hallucinated, one can make crucial interventions which will speed up the therapeutic process greatly. Of course, it is also essential that the patient has a sense of not being deserted, so it is extremely beneficial when there is continuity of contact. Therefore, anyone who wants to engage frequently in the treatment of acutely disturbed psychotics has to cultive a close relationship with a hospital that will permit him quick hospitalization and continued care of his own patient, both psychotherapeutically as well as psychopharmacologically.

Another aspect which may be even more difficult than the first two with regard to hospitalization is that it must be possible to get one's patients released from the hospital as promptly as possible. Ordinarily, administrative procedures may make it difficult to remove a patient from the hospital speedily. Yet, those patients who are suitable for ambulatory brief intensive psychotherapy could easily be harmed by the earlier-noted excessively long hospitalization which induces passivity and secondary gains from the hot house conditions of support and external controls.

4. A Family Network

This point is really an elaboration of the second one, namely the requirement that there be at least one person whom the therapist can address himself to, who will take some responsibility for the patient. If there is a whole *family network* available, this may play a crucial and beneficial role. Family network therapy has a definite and well-known place in treatment. Especially if inter-family pathology plays a marked role, it is essential to draw other family members into the therapeutic situation. This may be accomplished in different

80

ways. Indeed, one may choose to engage in either conjoint therapy with one other family member, or in family therapy per se. Under certain circumstances, the original therapist may wish to work with the entire family himself. In other instances, it may be more suitable to have other family members, or even the entire family, seen by another mental health professional. The two therapists must have the privilege of conferring with each other, so as to work as a team, even if not necessarily under the same roof.

5. An Auxiliary Therapist

The above point brings me to one of the less well-known and less practiced techniques, and that is the desirability of utilizing an *auxiliary therapist*, i.e., having two therapists treating the same patient simultaneously. The auxiliary therapist may be drawn in only during particularly stormy episodes. These may be due to an especially acute transference psychosis, or at times to a particular countertransference problem on the part of the primary therapist. The role of the auxiliary therapist is then to deal specifically with the transference psychotic phenomenon which may be too difficult for the patient, and maybe for the primary therapist, to handle directly. Meanwhile, the primary therapist continues to work on the problems that produced the acute transference psychosis.

Dyadic psychotherapy, especially in an office, can be a very lonely type of endeavor, fraught with all sorts of emotions, including anxiety for both therapist and patient. Therefore, it is often very useful to have, as a routine proviso, an auxiliary therapist who can dilute the transference and countertransference, if necessary. If one routinely works with acutely disturbed psychotics, it is often useful to introduce an auxiliary therapist early in the relationship, explaining to the patient that this colleague will be available should the primary therapist catch a cold, go on vacation, or otherwise be unavailable. Such availability, of course, is crucially important with the most highly disturbed people. This kind of arrangement is made more easily in a clinic or social agency than in private practice, but it is not impossible in the latter.

6. Awareness of Family and Community Resources

Especially for psychiatrists in private practice, it is important to be aware of all possible *resources in a patient's life (relatives, friends, etc.) and in the community*. Social workers and psychologists are more likely to be aware of these social support systems, such as social agencies, rehabilitation facilities, halfway houses, recreational facilities, and eventually vocational rehabilitation. It is important to make use of these facilities during treatment and certainly towards the end of treatment, when the patient needs a setting in which he can continue his improvement and recovery.

7. Hot-Lines and Emergency Centers

A variation on the theme of having access to an auxiliary therapist is the need to have easy access to *hot-lines and emergency centers*. Most communities, at this point, do have such services available, as part of their community facilities. These emergency services are usually listed on the inside cover of the phone book and, when they are properly administered, are accessible 24 hours a day. The telephone contact should be backed up by an available psychiatric emergency center in a clinic or social agency and, if possible, a mobile team which can visit a patient in his home and, in an extreme situation, commit and hospitalize him.

8. Do Not Be a Hero

I consider it extremely important to have *easy access to an alarm system*, in case a patient should become acutely disturbed and possibly dangerous. The ability to treat acutely disturbed people depends as much on the relative security of the setting within which therapy takes place, as on the therapist's capacity to tolerate feelings of anxiety and discomfort. Under any circumstances, *it is essential not to be inappropriately heroic*. The therapist should never allow situations to exist which are unduly dangerous in terms of his own safety. An anxious therapist can certainly not function effectively. An unsecured setting also makes the patient uneasy, because he may well fear his own possible loss of impulse control. Especially in large and active emergency treatment centers, it is best to have security personnel available. In settings which are less likely to have extremely disturbed patients, it is advantageous to have an office which is not located in too isolated a setting. It may be helpful to leave the door slightly ajar, provided that reasonable privacy is still retained. Again, such a provision is often also of benefit to the patient, who feels less frightened of the therapist and of his own impulses, when he perceives the situation as relatively secure.

9. Housing Situations

This point deals with a very difficult problem — the *suitability of the patient's housing situation*: namely, where the patient lives and where he or she should live for optimal improvement. The family setting is often extremely unhealthy and it may be almost impossible to do constructive therapeutic work in two or three hours a week if the remainder of the time there are forces within the family setting which are regressive and pathogenic. Therefore, it is essential, and certainly a major enabling condition, that if his present living situation is unsuitable then the patient must be moved to another setting. At first glance, this often appears to be impossible. I strongly suggest a very careful survey of all his relatives, friends and community resources, in an attempt to find a place for the patient to live and to sleep other than with his immediate family, if they are acutely pathogenic. If there are no appropriate relatives or friends, then foster homes or even half-way houses may be preferable, even though these facilities are often deleterious in their own way.

I cannot stress strongly enough the importance of a proper living situation for the patient, in order not to have the therapeutic process be more difficult than is necessary, or even to be rendered ineffective. I have found this factor, namely a healthy setting, to be so important, that if a patient of mine had a suitable family member living in another state, I was in favor of the patient moving to that other state, living with that family, and continuing with another therapist rather than myself.

10. Drugs

Finally, the use of *drugs* has to be mentioned as one very important enabling condition for engaging in psychotherapy with acutely disturbed psychotic patients. My favorite analogy of the role of medication in psychotherapy is that a drug plays the same role in facilitating the psychotherapeutic operation as an anesthetic does for a surgical intervention. It enables the doctor to engage in the often painful but necessary interventions, and still have a cooperative patient. Before general anesthetics were available, it was not only excessively traumatic, but often fatal, to perform an abdominal operation without properly relaxed musculature. A similar situation holds true for some psychotherapeutic interventions. Interpretations may be extremely painful and distressing for a patient — indeed, more than he can bear. This may provoke an episode of violence to himself or others, and lead to a more acute psychotic state. In other instances, without the benefit of psychotropic medication, the patient may be generally too anxious, too withdrawn, or too depressed to be either willing or able to communicate. Some patients may be terrified of approaching particular subject material which it is crucial to air and analyze. In such instances, drugs can be used to decrease "approach anxiety" or, as is the case of antidepressants, provide the patient with the "energy" to relate.

Caution must be observed not to medicate a patient to a point where most ego functions are interfered with and reality testing and the sense to self have been unduly affected by the psychotropic drug (14). It is undesirable to have a patient who feels foggy or "spaced out" — so lethargic as not to have any motivation for psychotherapeutic work. But it is, in fact, possible to choose one's drugs in such a way that some ego functions are improved, thereby facilitating the therapeutic process. Improvement of impulse control, e. g., of aggression, may be accomplished with lithium or phenothiazines. The latter may also improve thought processes, helping the patient to think logically and reason deductively — skills basic to his understanding therapeutic interpretations.

In summary, before initiating therapy with acutely disturbed psychotics, it is not only necessary to make a diagnosis in the narrow sense of the word, but also extremely important to evaluate all assets and liabilities in the patient's life situation. All difficulties which are likely to emerge in the process of treatment should be carefully assessed and planned for (17). Such accurate assessment and treatment design can serve to eliminate a great deal of trouble, waste and even tragedy.

However, if at least the minimal enabling conditions outlined above are met, the brief intensive ambulatory treatment of acutely disturbed psychotics may be a truly rewarding experience for both patient and therapist. In most instances, after the acute condition has been dealt with, it is desirable to engage in extensive psychoanalytic psychotherapy in order to deal with the patient's subtle structural, dynamic and characterological problems.

V.
The Intensive
BRIEF AND EMERGENCY PSYCHOTHERAPY
(B.E.P.)
of
ACUTE PSYCHOTIC STATES

V. ACUTE PSYCHOTIC STATES

THEORETICAL CONSIDERATIONS

Acute psychotics can often be treated very successfully by brief intensive psychotherapy, on an ambulatory basis if the nature of the disorder and the social setting of the patient permit (see Part II, Chapter IV) or as inpatients. This is one of the instances where intensive B. E. P. has a function in community psychiatry, by keeping many patients out of the hospital or in preventing chronicity by prompt intervention.

TEN SPECIFIC FACTORS IN THE
THERAPEUTIC MANAGEMENT
of
ACUTE PSYCHOTIC STATES

1. ESTABLISH CONTACT

2. ESTABLISH CONTINUITY

3. REASSURE BY UNDERSTANDING AND INTERPRETATION

4. STRUCTURE PATIENT'S LIFE

5. BE AVAILABLE

6. INVOLVE SIGNIFICANT OTHERS

7. SPLINTING

8. THERAPIST AS AUXILIARY EGO

9. DRUGS

10. BRIEF HOSPITALIZATION

1. Establish Contact

Acutely disturbed psychotics most frequently present in a panic state, and many of the points made in the discussion of panic states have application here (see Part II, Chapter IX). The psychotic patient in a panic is aware of something being wrong with him. New experiences — such as understanding the birds or feeling all powerful or possessing an incredible surge of energy or feeling oneself influenced by various forces — are frightening to the patient. He finds himself in a strange world. He has lost continuity and stives himself to recapture that continuity: e. g., paranoid ideation is one adaptive/maladaptive way the patient tries to make sense out of what ails him.

Many acute psychotics talk about having an "ah ha experience," a major feeling of revelation, which is another defensive attempt to make sense out of what is going on with them: they may suddenly feel that they are God or anointed by God or have undergone some other drastic change which would explain their psychotic phenomena.

It behooves the therapist, therefore, to *try to establish contact with the patient's psychotic thinking*, to throw him an anchor that will buoy him, make him feel more secure and understood. It is helpful if the therapist can interpret even a little, and let the patient know that he is with him, that he does not consider him beyond the pale. One may have to talk "schizophrenese" and enter into symbolisms, and thus establish some empathy. If this can be accomplished, one has done a great deal.

One patient pointed out that the radiator next to my chair was occasionally turning red. I was able to point out that he imagined this everytime he said or felt something angry, and that his perception of the radiator was his own awareness of turning red with anger. This interpretation considerably lowered the tension level and facilitated communication between us.

A young man who emphasized again and again that he had to be in a plaster cast for nine months was considerably relieved when I said: "Nevertheless, I know that you are a very masculine fellow." I was responding to the fact that nine months in a body cast referred to his feeling that he was a pregnant woman, and thus I reassured him indirectly of his masculinity. (Naturally, I had other information which supported the notion that he felt feminine and impregnated.)

2. Establish Continuity

Establishing continuity is very much part of the process discussed above, since the patient suffers from an experience of discontinuity. It is important to assure him that his delusions and hallucinations can make sense, and that his illness relates to certain life events, past or present; e. g., with a boisterous manic patient, that he started making himself feel big because he felt so small when he lost his job or had some other disturbing and belittling experience.

One can try and establish continuity not only between reality and hallucinations and delusions, but also between the patient's earlier history and his present symptomatology. One may point out to the patient that the voices he hears are actually the continued exhortations which he was accustomed to hear from mother or father (incidentally, these voices usually relate to maternal injunctions).

It is extremely important that one obtain from the patient — or from a relative or friend — information with regard to exactly what occurred prior to the manifest psychotic experience. A patient who suddenly believed that he was Jesus Christ and loved everyone had just had an enraging experience, and his delusion was an obvious attempt at denial of his rage. A woman patient who believed that everyone was watching her had just been "deserted" by her grown son, felt herself all alone, and *wished* that everyone would take an interest in her. A young college student who suddenly became delusional, believing that he was Christ, had become incoherent soon after he found a coed in his bed. The experience was too much for his superego and he stressed his asceticism psychotically.

If the therapist can ascertain and understand exactly what precipitated the psychotic break, he will be able to help the patient deal with his conflicts and anxieties.

3. Reassure by Understanding and Interpretation

Again, this third point relates closely to the first two above. Interpretations and evidence of understanding the patient go a long way toward establishing contact and providing him with the continuity he so anxiously misses. It reassures him to know that the therapist is not frightened by his symptomatology and will guide him through his psychotic "wilderness."

4. Structure the Patient's Life

Very often, an emotional overload has disorganized the patient's life. Some, like those suffering from an ADD Psychosis, may actually be primarily psychotic because they were overloaded and unable to structure life for themselves.

Schizophrenics may not possess enough synthetic ego function to "get their act together" and manics may be exercising denial and avoidance. It is therefore important to help the patient create a life situation which is bearable for him, both in terms of tasks to be accomplished and in terms of his actual living conditions. It may be necessary to advise the patient to move or otherwise find an appropriate place to live. The psychotic patient will usually need a rigid work schedule, as part of providing the structure that he lacks internally.

5. Be Available

The therapist must make himself available to the psychotic patient, since he is panicky and often unable to deal with ordinary day to day problems and feels himself easily overwhelmed. The patient gets a great deal of reassurance and strength in knowing that the therapist is available to him if necessary, even at night for a brief telephone conversation or on the weekend, should some emergency arise. It is essential that someone be there for the patient: if not the therapist himself, then hot lines or other emergency services may provide a useful function in this regard.

6. Involve Significant Others

This point relates to the above. Involving significant others will have the advantage of giving the patient a supportive network. As mentioned before, significant others can also be used in suicidal crisis, and may help change the ambiance of the situation within which the patient lives. Of course, one may have to help the significant others change in order to enable them to provide a different and better setting for the patient's life interactions.

7. "Splinting"

In recommending "splinting" for the therapeutic management of acute psychotics, I am taking the imagery from what a doctor would do for a dislocated or fractured arm or leg: temporarily easing the strain of it by support.

To ease the strain on a patient, one may have to suggest that he decrease his workload or eliminate or reduce whatever else it is in his life that is making excessive emotional, physical or other demands on him. In the case of an overworked housewife and mother, I might recommend a homemaker to ease her burdens. I will suggest whatever it takes to provide some rest and ease the strain on the patient, in order that the naturally healing forces of the ego have the chance to reconstruct themselves.

8. Therapist as Auxiliary Ego

Wherever the patient is really unable to resolve things for himself, the therapist should act as an auxiliary ego for him, in terms of reality testing, judgement, and even with concrete details of the patient's life. If the patient is unable to arrange an appropriate living and working situation for himself, then the therapist must function as his auxiliary ego for as long as is necessary, and help him to make these arrangements. Social workers may also be particularly helpful in this regard, and assist the patient in arranging for many practical, concrete aspects of his daily life.

9. Drugs

Drugs may be used as part of the enabling conditions for brief intensive psychotherapy with acute psychotics, or for enabling the patient to live in the community instead of being hospitalized while he is receiving ambulatory care.

The phenothiazines, haldoperidol, and other drugs are, of course, very often useful not only in treating the target conditions, which they often do only temporarily, but in creating the atmosphere within which psychotherapy can be carried out. My general use of certain drugs has often been misunderstood as a lack of dealing with target symptoms because, for example, I recommend either chlorpromazine or lithium for their aggression-controlling properties. Dynamically, one might want to use these drugs for their effect on drives, while using the barbiturates for a decrease of defenses. Lithium and chlorpromazine are more likely to inhibit aggression, while barbiturates like alcohol are more likely to decrease the defenses and release aggression or make it possible for the patient to communicate. Barbiturates may have their place in the treatment of mute catatonics in the form of pentothal interviews or even in oral or intra-muscular form. Ever since the widespread use of psychotropic drugs, the usefulness of barbiturates has mostly been forgotten.

10. Brief Hospitalization

As discussed under Enabling Conditions (see Part II, Chapter IV), the energetic ambulatory psychotherapy of acute psychotics may necessitate brief episodes of hospitalization. What has been said in that chapter holds true here.

VI.

The Intensive

BRIEF AND EMERGENCY PSYCHOTHERAPY
(B. E. P.)
of
PHYSICAL ILLNESS OR SURGERY

VI. PHYSICAL ILLNESS OR SURGERY

CONCEPTUAL CONSIDERATIONS

Brief intensive psychotherapy, very often in the form of emergency psychotherapy, plays an important role in all of liaison psychiatry, and especially in cases of physical illness and surgery.

The need for B. E. P. may arise in various forms and in various stages of an Ilness. B. E. P. may be used upon request for a consultation by a physician or by the patient. It may be indicated with a patient who is in a panic when informed of a possible malignancy, or when told of the necessity for a surgical procedure. Brief psychotherapeutic intervention may be necessary preoperatively or postoperatively, or at the point where a physical illness or sequalae from surgery have become a chronic, psychiatrically incapacitating disorder.

Certain basic principles hold true here as elsewhere: It is essential to understand the nature of the problem in terms of the patient's general life history. The specific meaning of the illness or surgery for each individual patient must be explored and judiciously illuminated.

Some general principles are useful to keep in mind: The impact of frightening experiences may be met with denial, to be followed by a depression, or they may be met with an immediate reactive anxiety or depression. On the other hand, the threat may not be responded to with any manifest emotional reaction, but rather translate itself into psychosomatic or chronic psychiatric form, or lead to poor healing or lack of conformance with medical instructions.

Some illness, especially chronic illness, may be responded to with *anthropomorphization*. During the course of the illness, a relationship is often established between the patient and his diseased organ similar to that of a parent to a child. The diseased organ may take on the role of the sick child who needs care. This is apparent in phrases like "My stomach can't tolerate . . ." Or the organ may take on the characteristics of a tyrannical parent: "My liver won't let me eat that." The diseased organ may be first anthropomorphized and then spoken of as having an independent life, with independent preferences and sensitivities.

Illness affects changes in the self image, the body image, and in the organ image, and all of these changes need to be explored. In chronic illness, a whole "organization" of defenses may take place, and one can study the accretions like the rings of a tree. In such a case, the goals of brief intensive psychotherapy have to be chosen judiciously: A chronic migraine headache may be the symptomatic expression of a lifelong isolation which is too much to face in an irreversible life situation and is best left alone. Generally supportive measures might be the best choice in the treatment of such a person.

A tremendous literature has developed on the topic of the psychological care of the terminally ill and should certainly be kept in mind when engaging in B. E. P. with this group of patients.

In the case of impending surgery, the therapist should explore the patient's general and specific fears of surgery. The fears of dying by surgery may differ from the fears of dying in general. Notions of being cut open are taken from both childhood fantasies and unfortunate real life experiences, for example, a particularly traumatic tonsillectomy as a child.

Surgery is a psychological as well as a physical trauma. In this type of crisis situation, the therapist is often called upon to act as liaison between the patient, his family, the surgeon, and the participating hospital staff. He can serve as displacement for the anxieties of all involved, and can help open paths of communication that otherwise might remain closed. Though the therapist should involve himself with all aspects of this crisis situation, his primary emphasis will be on the patient and the patient's family.

The therapist cannot replace the primary physician in the eyes of the patient. However, a sufficient knowledge of surgical procedures provides a basis for communication. The patient often is reluctant to discuss certain aspects of surgery with his surgeon, including any ambivalence he may have, due to the fact that he is dependent upon the surgeon for his life. The therapist therefore can help enlighten the patient about areas he might otherwise be unwilling to discuss.

Surgeons may appear overly optimistic about the proposed surgery, or will not divulge certain unpleasant aspects of the operation for fear of discouraging or frightening the patient and his family. The therapist seeing a preoperative patient in hospital is dealing with a crisis situation even though the patient may not be aware that there is a crisis. The area of patient-therapist confidentiality is modified by agreement under these circumstances to include, inform, and prepare everyone concerned. Thus they become affective participants in the patient's experience with surgery.

The patient's expectations about the surgery and its aftereffects are valuable clues to the therapist. He should develop a strong preoperative relationship with the patient. The patient is medically better prepared to face surgery if he is psychologically prepared beforehand. The therapist's supportive and educational role is strengthened if he leaves his phone number with the patient.

The experience after surgery of waking up in an intensive care unit — disoriented, fatigued, immobilized, surrounded by machines, possibly in severe pain, and completely dependent on others — is frightening even when the patient has been prepared. It is important that the patient be informed as to how he will feel upon awakening. The postoperative environment of the intensive care unit should also be discussed in detail. By being able to orient himself in space and time, the patient is less likely to react psychotically;

94

"structures" such as a clock, calendar, and windows lend themselves to proper reorientation. In a similar way, the therapist becomes the supportive link between the preoperative and postoperative experience.

Should the patient's need for continued medical service cause tensions between him and his family or the participating hospital staff, the therapist can serve as a vehicle for the clarification and resolution of anxieties or conflicts.

In situations where postoperative psychoses occur, the therapist must consider possible physical contributing factors of toxic nature. Dislike of the patient by the staff may affect him and also contribute to a postoperative psychosis.

In the fragile patient, the therapist's continued support is important in the postoperative phase, and should include follow-up visits. If any conflict or discomfort persists, the surgeon and the patient's family can be called in to further support and encourage the patient.

TEN SPECIFIC FACTORS IN THE
THERAPEUTIC MANAGEMENT
of
PHYSICAL ILLNESS OR SURGERY

1. EXPLORE THE PATIENT'S CONCEPT OF THE ILLNESS OR IMPENDING SURGERY

2. EXPLORE THE PERSONAL MEANING AND ROLE OF THE ILLNESS (SECONDARY GAINS, ETC.)

3. EDUCATE THE PATIENT

4. ESTABLISH CONTACT WITH TREATING PHYSICIAN OR SURGEON

5. EXPLORE THE MEANING OF ANESTHESIA

6. SPECIFIC NOTIONS AND FEARS OF DEATH

7. SPECIFIC TYPES OF ILLNESS AND SURGERY

8. ORGANS OF SEXUAL SIGNIFICANCE

9. MALIGNANCIES

10. HEART DISEASE

1. Explore the Patient's Concept of the Illness or Impending Surgery

The specific meaning of the illness or surgery to the patient must be identified and insight achieved therapeutically. Thus a male patient's identification of his illness with the illness of his mother may lead to false conscious expectations and pathogenic female identification. A tuberculosis patient may need to be shown that his conception of the bleeding hole in his lung actually reveals childhood conceptions of female genitalia and castration. Dreams may provide concrete details that will make it quite easy to interpret such unconscious material. Of course, the therapist's style of language when interpreting this material needs to be suitably simple.

Narcissistic injury often plays a major role. In a woman, this could manifest itself in a concern with beauty, and in a man, a concern with "machismo." In each case, the illness needs to be analyzed with regard to both the realistic and the symbolic meaning.

Often, the affected organ becomes overcathected in the course of an illness. When the liver becomes diseased, for example, it will tend to loom very large in the patient's body image, like the New Yorker's concept of the United States which envisions the city covering two-thirds of the map. This conceptual distortion can be easily demonstrated if the therapist asks the patient to draw the body, including the affected organ or part (48).

Having the patient draw pictures of his bodily affliction will help to clarify his concept of it: He might draw a picture of a coronary with an embolus in the artery that looks like a phallus attacking it. He might draw a picture of a malignancy that looks like a gaping mouth with teeth, revealing cannibalistic fantasies about the malignancy.

One patient, who was terribly disgusted by the idea of having a gastric ulcer, reacted with nausea to the idea of having fluid oozing in his stomach. He found the gastric ulcer particularly unappetizing because he equated it with the leg ulcers he had seen on an aging relative.

2. Explore the Personal Meaning and Role of the Illness (Secondary Gains, Etc.)

A phenomenon characteristic of all psychopathology and a common ally to organic illness is *secondary gain*. Gaining attention, avoiding responsibility, controlling and tyrannizing the family, and similar means of capitalizing on and exploiting illness are all too familiar and can be seen most dramatically in "insurance neurosis," or "pension syndrom," where illness has brought some advantage to the patient and may operate unconsciously to retard his recovery. Thus an investigation of the patient's anxieties must include an examination of the superficial meaning that the illness holds for him, as well as the factors that derive from earlier notions that have been deeply repressed and find contemporary representation in psychic overlay.

Enforced passivity, especially of a lengthy nature, may pose a dire threat to one patient and for another patient, represent an infantile gratification which he makes the most of.

Specific operations may be particularly threatening to some people for idiosyncratic reasons. For example, a female patient became psychotic after a hemorrhoidectomy. This patient had been able to have orgasms only by anal stimulation. Hemorrhoidectomy was seen as a sexual act as well as a terrible threat to her sexuality. Postoperative delusions and hallucinations in this and similar instances usually involve the surgeon and frequently have a paranoid flavor.

3. Educate the Patient

The structure of the patient's unconscious, preconscious, or even conscious notion of his injury or illness should be established through the history, often with the aid of projective techniques such as the Draw-A-Person Test and Thematic Appreception Test. With these misconceptions identified, the therapist may initiate a period of education. For instance, a discussion of the anatomy of a coronary and anastomotic repair (with a comparison to the healing of a fractured arm bone) may vastly improve the patient's body image.

An educated patient is often the most cooperative. Lack of compliance with medication or other treatment is often the result of a lack of understanding by the patient. If the primary care physician does not fulfill the role of the "educator," it becomes the psychotherapist's task to enlighten the patient and gain this variety of therapeutic alliance.

4. Establish Contact with Treating Physician or Surgeon

It is best not to be at cross-purposes with the hospital personnel. Therefore, the therapist should clear his professional visits with the administration and, as a professional courtesy, with the surgeon and internist on the case. If surgeons are particularly worried about the patient's mental condition, and/or if they have had some experience with psychotherapy themselves, they may have a relatively enlightened view of the therapist's visits. However, surgeons are at times narcissistic and concrete in their thinking, even vis-a-vis other physicians.

If the psychotherapist is perceived as "helper" by the other physicians, his role will be facilitated. In order to be most effective, the therapist will often have to acquaint himself with the intricacies of special medical or surgical conditions.

5. Explore the Meaning of Anesthesia

Not to be overlooked is the need to explore the patient's specific fears concerning anesthesia. Many such fears can arise and may be extremely troubling. Thus, patients fear sensations of choking, burning in the throat and lungs struggling for air. Some people prefer spinal anesthesia because they would rather remain awake to keep an eye on things, including their surgeon. They may feel better staying conscious as a reflection of concerns about perhaps not waking up again, or especially strong fears of passivity. Other people don't want to know and prefer intravenous sedation followed by inhalation anesthesia.

The therapist should be familiar with the preoperative procedures, including sedation, and with the types of anesthesia available. The therapist and patient should urge the surgeon to commit himself concerning the procedures and anesthetics, thus permitting therapist and patient to anticipate particular anxieties. The anesthesiologist should discuss the choices of anesthesia prior to the surgery. Occasionally, for instance, pre-anesthesia is given rectally; some patients are more upset by this than by the surgery itself.

With modern anesthetics, waking up after surgery is not necessarily un-pleasant. If possible, it is helpful to have someone familiar in the room when the patient awakens. Waking up in an intensive care unit, disoriented, fatigued, immobilized, possibly in pain, and completely dependent on others, is a frightening experience, even when the patient is prepared for it. The post-operative environment of the ICU should be discussed in detail. Being able to orient himself, the patient is less likely to react with panic as he awakens from anesthesia. At least when the patient returns to his room, someone familiar should be there to comfort him. The therapist himself can become the supportive link between the preoperative and postoperative states.

Note: With regard to the fear of anesthesia, I have noted that frequently a childhood experience with a tonsillectomy has remained a very traumatic memory: the feeling of suffocating under the ether mask, the sensation of something fiery, some recollection of struggling, is the fearful model for many.

6. Specific Notions and Fears of Death

As noted earlier, contrary to what one might expect, death has quite different meanings to different people. For many, it signifies loneliness: "alone in a cold grave"; for others, it involves envy of others who will go on to reap pleasures after the deceased is gone. More idiosyncratically, some dread being devoured by worms, others that they may be buried alive with the accompanying claustrophobic anxieties. One woman was greatly troubled by the idea that she would lie nude and exposed on the undertaker's table. Another patient feared that her "drawers" might be found untidy.

The process of dying may be dreaded as a form of torture, or primarily due to a fear of loss of control. In each patient preoccupied with his particular fear of death and dying, it is essential to explore the specific meaning of the fear.

There is at present a vast literature available on how to deal with the dying patient, and it behooves the therapist to acquaint himself with it.

7. Specific Types of Illness and Surgery

Statistically, abdominal operations were (until the advent of open heart surgery) seen as the major surgical threat and had the highest incidence of postoperative psychoses. The therapist must explore the patient's fantasies about what procedures will be performed in the abdomen. Amputations are high on the list of procedures which precipitate psychoses, as are dialysis and diabetes.

With regard to dialysis, having one's lifeblood course through a kind of laundramat-device, is understandably frightening. Toxic conditions, for which the dialysis is undertaken, often contribute to typical features of an organic psychosis.

Severe diabetes, especially the juvenile type, is one of the conditions which is accompanied by special problems with regard to patients' compliance. The complications of sometimes slipping into acidosis or severe hypoglycemia have a life threatening quality which needs to be specifically worked through with the patient.

8. Organs of Sexual Significance

Illness or surgery involving the sexual organs takes on particular significance because of the special libidinous social and moral role played by sexuality. The venereal diseases, of course, have a special place. While the "leper complex" concerning syphiles has decreased with the advent of penicillin, genital herpes has now attained that status. Guilt over promiscuity may play a prominent role, conception of dirtiness another. Rage and even paranoid reactions may be triggered.

Afflicitions of the penis and vagina are, of course, of great concern. An ovarectomy may involve misconceptions on the part of the patient, and even a hysterectomy without an ovarectomy may often be perceived or experienced as a form of castration. Instrumental manipulation and examination, such as catheterization or cystoscopy or tubal inflation are all likely to carry a good deal of irrational notions with them.

Specific kinds of surgery to sexual organs stimulate rather standard reactions. A prostate operation will usually arouse fears of impotence and reawaken old castration anxieties. Breast operations, on the other hand, are often perceived as threats to a patient's femininity. Legitimate concerns about the cosmetic aspects, as well as possible complications of the operation, need to be discussed with the patient.

9. Malignancies

Professional intervention in the case of an individual with a diagnosed malignancy generally follows one or two procedures. The first allows the patient to respond and adjust to his condition in his own way, with the aid of the therapist who strives only to enhance the adaptive response. The second procedure applies to instances in which the patient cannot deal with the monumental crisis of terminal illness and engages in massive denial. In both instances, the patient is permitted to take the lead, although he should always be able to feel the supportive presence of the therapist. The therapist should discuss medical advances with the patient without inappropriately raising his hopes for survival. He can help educate the patient about the nature of his illness, and anticipate his questions to help ease his anxiety, or help him discuss treatment priorities. In many of the better hospitals there is excellent liaison between the oncology and psychiatry services.

Again, the specific subjective meaning of the malignancy must be identified. For some cancer patients, the oral aggressive features of the patient's personality may find exaggeration in the disease so that they perceive the cancer as an eating, boring, destroying phenomenon. With others in whom the sado-masochistic features are predominant, the cancer may be perceived as a brutal, sadistic, attacking introject. In a similar fashion, the specific meaning of the death must be dealt with. All that has been said before about the fears of death and dying have to be kept in mind here. The problem of denial is not only of special concern with regard to the patient and his relatives, but also for the oncologist, surgeon and the therapist himself.

The countertransference problems to moribund patients are tremendous and emotionally exhausting. It takes careful self-analysis in every instance to function optimally and only with the irreducible degree of pain and anxiety.

10. Heart Disease

The heart has a special symbolic and emotional significance, aside from its vital realistic one.

Heart patients are often frightened and depressed by their brush with death. They should be given a full understanding and prognosis of their condition with as much optimism as possible. Coronary patients, especially young ones, who feel less mortally threatened and consequently less vulnerable, should not be smothered with reassurances which might prove more harmful than beneficial. The younger heart patient often is not readily able to assimilate what has happened to him. In this case intervention may involve interpretation of denial without unduly frightening the patient.

The therapist must anticipate the patient's feeling of depression following discharge from the hospital, and be prepared to take a supportive role in the follow-up treatment. The patient who is informed that he may weaken and tire easily following a heart attack will be in a far better position to cope with these symptoms should they develop after this return to his home and family. The therapist should encourage the patient to follow an exercise program prescribed by his physician, or to be sure an exercise program has been prescribed. Many heart patients are reluctant to tax themselves physically, but the therapist can help overcome the patient's fears by pointing out that appropriate activity in fact strengthens the heart. Thus the therapist can help the patient avoid becoming a chronic invalid because of excessive fear and passivity.

Heart disease has certain unique sequelae: It is experienced, at first, as a severe threat to life, associated as it is with sudden death. Misconception about the diagnosis itself — for example, confusion of rheumatic heart disease with coronary disease — can result in inappropriate fear. More frequently, however, intrapsychic factors that have their dynamic roots in repressed fear of powerlesness, abandonment, and castration and which are now reawakened, account for the incapacitating fear of death.

Whereas the amputee, for example, does not often think of work as impairing his health, the cardiac patient frequently focuses on work as a hazard. His overwhelming fear that any exertion may shorten his life poses a special problem in his psychotherapy and especially in his rehabilitation. On the other hand, a cardiac patient with a defensive need to deny his illness may be self-destructive — for example, the patient who insists on pushing a piano around.

By the very nature of the organ involved, cardiac illness poses another unique problem. The heart is the symbol of basic human emotions — love, affection, and hatred — and therefore holds the position of primacy among all body organ. The cardiovascular system is a special participant in affective syndromes; arrhythmia, tachycardia, and dyspnea are somatic equivalents of anxiety and need not be referable to heart disease. Psychosomatic studies have shown that the cardiovascular system can respond to stress situations with increased heart rate, rise in systolic pressure, and increase in cardiac output. Physiological changes and disturbances in autonomic rhythm can in turn create apprehension and set in motion a psychosomatic circuit that challenges the most perceptive diagnostic skills. With anxiety manifestations that stimulate cardiac symptoms, and chronic tension states that effect internal physiological responses, the diagnostic problem created understandably adds nourishment to the hypochondriacal concerns of the cardiac patient.

Another problem that contributes to the disproportionate disability of some cardiac patients are the iatrogenic factors. Physicians are likely to contribute more to the invalidism of the cardiac patient than to that of any other type of patient. This is probably related to the fact that as a group physicians are more likely than the general population to develop heart disease, and tend on the whole to be extremely apprehensive about having a coronary episode. They are apt to project onto their patients their own anxieties according to their own psychological needs and to advise their patients to be unduly restrictive.

Bellak and Haselkorn (13) found that patients with a premorbid history of overcompensatory, competitive, aggressive behavior (used as a denial against excessive underlying passivity) appeared more emotionally threatened by coronary disease. For these patients, outlets for discharge of anxiety in excessive activity were denied by the cardiac disease. The resulting psychic conflict contributed further to the somatopsychological problem.

Open-heart surgery frequently stimulates severe emotional problems. Because of the heart's function in sustaining life, the images of it stopping, of it being lifted out of the chest, of being attached to an artificial heart, all intensify the question of life and death for the patient. Many patients fear brain damage because of the long period of anesthesia that open-heart surgery requires. The chest-long incision, and the image of the ribs being sawed, dramatically affects the body image. Indeed, delirious episodes after open-heart surgery are not rare.

VII.
The Intensive
BRIEF AND EMERGENCY PSYCHOTHERAPY
(B. E. P.)
of
CATASTROPHIC LIFE EVENTS

VII. CATASTROPHIC LIFE EVENTS

THEORETICAL CONSIDERATIONS

The understandable impulse in dealing with someone suffering from the impact of a catastrophic event or experience is to focus on the immediate event. The fact is, of course, that this event also has to be seen in the context of the person's entire life experience, and its specific meaning explored. The contemporary event has to be understood in terms of its apperceptive distortions by all previous life events, as any catastrophic event will have different meanings for different people.

As in all acute situations, a certain amount of tact is appropriate. Somebody who has just suffered a loss of a close relative or been in a serious accident is not someone to whom one should interpret. Nor should a history be elicited immediately. Some understanding, emotional support, and the promise of future help is appropriate for a start.

When the circumstances permit, one has to attempt to see the catastrophic reaction in relation to the person's life situation and in relation to the precipitating event. For instance, the Viet Nam veteran discussed in the appendix certainly had horrifying experiences in combat and seemingly had every reason to have recurrent nightmares from the stress of the danger of attack in Viet Nam. Nevertheless, the specific form that this fear of *guerrilla* attacks took was predicated upon his earlier fear of the mother whom he dreamt of in childhood as a *gorilla* attacking him. In this man's case, the whole catastrophic experience of Viet Nam must be seen in terms of his struggle with passivity and aggression in his earlier life.

Even with concentration camp victims, it has been quite clear that the impact of their dreadful experiences were, to a large extent, affected by their previous life experiences and personality structure. By and large, those who had well adjusted lives previously managed to bear the bestialities of the Nazis better than those who had a traumatic life history.

In dealing with victims of single traumatic events, one has to keep in mind different phases of response in the victim. This was pointed out by Friedman and Linn (26) in connection with their study of survivors of the *Andrea Doria* disaster. They speak of the initial psychic shock, a variety of pathological responses and distortions, and the recovery phase. Similar observations are made by Hilberman in connection with rape (29).

TEN SPECIFIC FACTORS RE: CATASTROPHIC LIFE EVENTS

1. CATHARSIS

2. SPECIFIC MEANING OF EVENT

3. EXPLORATION OF "LIABILITY" AND GUILT

4. CHRONIC SEQUAELAE

5. SPECIFIC RESPONSES TO JOB LOSS AND RETIREMENT

6. SPECIFIC RESPONSES TO LOSS THROUGH DEATH: BEREAVEMENT

7. SPECIFIC RESPONSES TO MUGGING AND BURGLARY

8. SPECIFIC RESPONSES TO RAPE

9. SPECIFIC RESPONSES TO ACCIDENTS

10. SPECIFIC RESPONSES TO ECOLOGICAL THREATS

1. Catharsis

Catharsis is an interesting concept. It means, literally, a cleaning out or purging, and one must expect that the symbolism is taken from the digestive tract. Freud engaged in cathartic treatment very early in his career, when he still used suggestion and hypnosis, and had patients relive certain events in order to manage them emotionally. This treatment was predicated on the notion that upsetting events are often suppressed or repressed. Indeed, this concept is sometimes spoken of critically as his "hydraulic model," a model predicated upon the contemporary "Zeitgeist" of Helmholtz and Boltzman: it was assumed that suppressed energy dissipated by being made conscious would not cause trouble anymore. Many have criticized the model on theoretical grounds. Psychoanalysis, in fact, has come to rely on the much more sophisticated structural model and on the interpretation of defenses.

The fact is, however, that the concept of catharsis has remained clinically useful. It was widely used in front line psychiatry during the Second World War, and was the underlying concept in the therapeutic management of crash pilots. With the help of sodium pentothal intravenously, they were given a chance to work through the traumatic experience and in that way "wash it out of their system." A variety of current faddist "therapies" are based primarily on catharsis. The idea of the "primal scream" is based on the idea of "getting it out of one's system." The regrettable fact is that catharsis alone is usually not sufficient to produce real change. It leads, at best, to a temporary relief which is usually soon followed by a recurrence of the symptoms or new symptoms unless other dynamic interventions are also used in tandem (9).

Nevertheless, within the context of a sophisticated therapeutic approach, catharsis can play a significant role. At a point where the patient has recovered from the most immediate impact of a catastrophic life experience, it may indeed be worthwhile to have him relive the event in order to avoid denial or repression and to provide a chance for him to emote. There may be a great deal of rage, appropriate or inappropriate, which should be expressed. Appropriate mourning is important to engage in. Guilt feelings might be suitably expressed.

It is the task of the therapist to help the patient ventilate, to engage in catharsis, and only after that, to turn to other therapeutic maneuvers. This requires tact as well as appropriate timing, so that the catharsis will be optimally useful.

2. Specific Meaning of Event

Whatever crisis brings the patient to therapy, it is important to try to understand the impact of the contemporary crisis in terms of the patient's life situation. One accident victim may respond by primarily feeling a threat to his ability to be in control, while another will have fears of mutilation or problems of narcissism. The word "primarily" deserves special attention: Each crisis usually involves five or six basic factors whose rank order of importance will vary from person to person so that an overriding factor in one person will be of minimal importance in another.

The therapist should be generally knowledgeable about the factors *generally* relevant for each crisis; without general propositions we have no science. In this sense, the psychotherapist uses the knowledge and rules of his profession much as the surgeon uses the guidelines for the optimal sequence of surgical interventions: anatomical areas and structures to be dealt with, physiological considerations concerning stress, and complicating factors.

Jacobson and his colleagues (32) at the Benjamin Rush Institute identified the *generic* and the *individual* approaches to crisis as guides to the application of interventions. The generic concept holds that each type of crisis provokes its own unique patterns of response. The individual concept embraces the importance of the bio-psycho-social events in the individual's life. At the same time that a general frame of reference is utilized, the therapist must be flexible by adapting to and conceptually incorporating the individual responses of each patient that derive from his personal bio-psycho-social past.

For instance, being the subject of a divorce action is likely to involve feelings of rejection and problems of separation. For one husband, his wife's bringing suit — rather than both partners agreeing that lawyers negotiate conditions — meant to him that she did not trust him to be fair and reasonable. His personal concern with feelings of trustworthiness and honesty provoked a severe crisis, so that it was necessary to understand why this contemporary event produced such intense concern about his trustworthiness. What life history factors caused him to perceive the situation in this particular way? The usual feelings of rejection and separation were secondary to this question.

Although many crisis-producing events will cut dynamically across these lines, most critical life situations may be grouped under three headings: those that involve violence and arouse fears for one's life, health and sense of self; the loss of self-esteem; and the loss of love or of loved ones.

A serious accident, mugging, or rape; a serious illness or death-threatening incident; or the disorganizing effect of hallucinogenic drugs may all arouse fears about one's sense of self, frequently accompanied by feelings of depersonalization and fears of regressive disorganization. Those crises provoking loss of self-esteem and the experience of rejection or separation include job loss, divorce, an unhappy love affair, financial reverses, and aging, among others.

Medical and surgical problems often cut across these lines and involve fears of death, incapacity, and disfiguration. Certain situations such as abortion and decisions about heroic methods of life support systems are likely to stimulate conflicts involving conscience, aggression, and identification.

Hospitalization often produces a crisis in self-esteem which has been vividly described by both physicians and patients (44). Suddenly one is a unit to be moved, turned, injected, exposed, and at times treated callously enough to elicit intense anxiety, anger, or depression. Severe physical conditions such as malignancies, cardiac conditions, or neurological afflictions often evoke unique distortions and anxieties.

3. Exploration of "Liability" and Guilt

The experience of unconscious guilt is a wide-spread phenomenon, which can be traced back to ancient times. When an earthquake or a destructive thunderstorm occurred, the ancients and primitives immediately interpreted it as the anger of the Gods, an anger presumably the result of their having sinned in some way. They then tried to assuage their guilt by appeasing the Gods through various kinds of sacrifice.

This primitive, non-specific unconscious sense of guilt plays a role in most everyone's life, and in some people, excessively so. In general, the stricter the individual's upbringing, the more likely it is that he will feel a general sense of being "bad," some feelings of guilt related to sexual or aggressive thoughts, and some masochistic features will generally also be present.

Very often then, these features will attach themselves to an intercurrent event, and the unfortunate victim of some catastrophe will complicate his life and make things worse for himself by attaching free-floating guilt feelings to the event. He will feel, "If I had only turned left instead of right, the car accident would not have happened," even though objectively it may not at all be the victim's fault and circumstances were completely beyond his control. In one case, a man who had properly stopped his car at the stop sign was hit sideways by an oncoming vehicle. Nevertheless, he tortured himself with feeling that he should not have gone out at the time of day that he did to buy something which, in retrospect, he considered "frivolous." He blamed himself especially for some injury that his son had suffered in that accident: feeling a variety of "survivor guilt" is especially frequent. In the same vein, a coronary embolism may be blamed on dietary indulgence, and a rape on having dressed too seductively.

In each instance, it is important to find out what, if any, unconscious guilt feelings may be involved in the response to a catastrophic event, in order to relieve them as promptly as possible.

4. Chronic Sequaelae

Any catastrophic event, especially if it has not been "worked through," may lead to a variety of chronic disturbances. The pioneering paper on this subject, involving large numbers of people, was that of E. Lindemann (37).

He examined the survivors and relatives of victims of the Boston Coconut Grove Fire, and found that those who had used denial as a defense mechanism and had failed to work through the event, were likely to suffer a high incidence of psychosomatic disturbances, as well as neurotic symptoms, depression and other psychiatric disturbances, often rekindling childhood anxieties. The importance of working through has also been recognized in connection with rape (see later). Serious social withdrawal, phobias and sexual problems often derive from the rape experience.

The delayed, continued effect of catastrophic events on Viet Nam veterans is at present still an issue, even more than a decade after the last soldier came home. Their chronic sequaelae are a major concern to psychiatrists who are treating these veterans in the V. A. hospitals and elsewhere.

There is probably no concentration camp victim who has not been left with permanent scars from his catastrophic experience, though to varying degrees: in part related to the nature of his particular experience, and in part to his pre-existing personality structure, and other circumstances.

Therefore, it is important in the case of catastrophic events to help the patient deal with the acute experience by working through, via catharsis, support, and any other appropriate therapeutic measures in order to minimize the continued chronic sequaelae.

5. Job Loss and Retirement

A loss is a loss is a loss, to paraphrase Gertrude Stein. A job loss is no exception. For this reason, all the dynamics discussed under depression in relation to a loss (See page 54) are relevant here, including the decrease in self-esteem, the feeling of having been deceived, the aspect of disappointment, and the rage that is engendered along with these feelings.

Obviously, job loss involves far more than just a financial threat. In our culture, a person is largely defined by the job he holds. A job means a certain role, an identity and a certain place in a hierarchy. A job provides a clearly defined structure, which most people need. We need a place to go in the morning, a place to leave at night, and specific tasks to perform. Without structure, many people feel hopelessly lost. Most jobs, within their context, support significant aspects of self-esteem. Other aspects of self-esteem and role are further supported by a job in relation to a patient's family and friends. The "pater familias" who is accustomed to bringing home the bacon finds himself seriously and broadly threatened by a job loss.

In fact, job loss has become recognized as a serious enough issue or trauma to have prominent business firms design a personnel program especially for people that they have to discharge. It is euphemistically called "The placing-out program." The about-to-be-discharged employee is given access to psychological counseling, and help with other aspects of relocating or restructuring his or her life. There are a number of large firms dedicated to providing precisely this service of smoothing the "out-placing" and helping with resettlement and reorientation.

In the B. E. P. of Job Loss, the therapist, as mentioned above, should address himself to the problems of self-esteem, change of role, etc., according to their rank importance in each individual.

With regard to the problems of retirement: There is at present a population of more than 25 million people of an age over 65. The Social Security Act of 1935 had defined that age as the retirement age because many people usually felt old at that point. Today, however, not only has life expectancy increased, but, more importantly, a very large percentage of people over age 65 remain in perfect mental and physical health, in distinction to earlier decades, and do not really need or want to idle their time away in an induced invalidism.

The net result of these and other factors is that retirement is often a form of severe dislocation and upset. The person suddenly loses status, the structure of his everyday life, and he loses at least some income. Enlightened firms now offer some counseling programs with regard to retirement, but the fact is that the overwhelming majority of people still don't give it too much thought until it has come upon them. And it often does come upon them with catastrophic ferocity. Some will react with a depression, others with physical or psychosomatic ailments. Some will move to retirement homes, such as those in the sun-belt. Unfortunately, that often means that they also lose all their accustomed social ties, and suffer feelings of displacement.

Retirement problems are, of course, often as much sociologic and economic as they are psychological. There is a young work force that wants to replace the older one, and no individual therapy will deal effectively with the problem. It will take social action to really make a difference.

Meanwhile, each person affected by retirement has to deal with it in terms of his individual circumstances. Certainly, those who plan, anticipate, and arrange for their retirement are much better prepared for it and do best during it than those individuals who simply drift toward it. In general, the patient should be helped to structure and manage his new time schedule. The degree of structure that each person needs to establish and maintain will vary; the therapist should discuss these needs with the patient and help him to establish a schedule and activities which are best suited to his needs. Most people are conditioned over the years to equate work with monetary reward. The therapist can help the retired patient shift the emphasis from monetary reward; in retirement, work can more fully be equated with pleasure. The therapist may want to suggest sources for activity, such as acting as foster grandparents and numerous other volunteer activities. If the patient wishes to, and is physically able to work for a salary, he should be encouraged to do so. However, the therapist should be alert to the retired patient's feeling of loss of identity as a possible reason for seeking paid work. If this is the patient's major reason for seeking paid work, the therapist should help the patient establish a newer, or another aspect of his identity, through diverse and pleasurable activities.

6. Loss Through Death: Bereavement

The loss of a loved one is a severe catastrophy in a variety of ways. It is a loss which interrupts the continuity of one's life, that is, the essential basis of daily functioning. The bereaved person has to adapt to this loss of continuity of the relationship with the deceased. It is a traumatic reminder of one's own vulnerability and mortality. In addition, it often disrupts one's social, financial, and emotional network. In the case of loss of a spouse, it suddenly changes one's relationship to a large number of people to whom one had related as a couple.

All these and many other aspects of bereavement involve, indeed, "working through," i.e., a new adaptation, becoming accustomed to a new situation, finding other modes of relating. In addition, one has to come to terms with one's feelings for the deceased. The more ambivalent the feelings, the more difficult the struggle is, since the aggressive and negative feelings produce guilt. Some rage about being left by the deceased and saddled with the myriad problems arising therefrom is inevitable, and also needs to be dealt with.

In the case of the loss of a child, the identification with it and with one's hopes and expectations, and the loss of a tremendous emotional investment are severe blows.

The therapist should not actively intervene in the work of mourning as long as the patient himself is performing it. He enters into the dynamics of the bereavement only after some of the acuteness has worn off and the patient seems to need help, and then only at a carefully measured pace. When therapeutic intervention is indicated, the areas requiring exploration include the reaction to object loss, the particular meaning of the object relation to the departed, superego reactions, and, as mentioned before, feelings of loss, of disappointment, of rage and helplessness.

In the cases of loss of aged parents, a process frequently referred to as "preliminary mourning" may well have taken place and decreased the acuteness of the reaction. As one abserves an aging person losing their health, their competence, one slowly withdraws emotional investment and mourns the *partial loss* of the competent and meaningful person the parent had been. This is important to keep in mind, so as not to confuse it with denial or lack of working through.

If mourning a parent is done properly, a person may actually emerge with greater individuation. In our culture, or at least our past culture, the loss of a father often enables a son to do the final maturing, to come into his own.

If the work of mourning is not done well, it turns into a depression and all the factors discussed under depression (see page 51) should then be addressed.

7. Specific Responses to Mugging and Burglary

Five houses were burglarized in my neighborhood under similar circumstances. One neighbor who has in general a good adaptation to life did not feel personally threatened and dealt appropriately with the incident. Another neighbor talked of it frequently. He elaborated a distinct fantasy in which he would set a trap for the next intruder. The burglar would fall through a trapdoor and be impaled on spikes. This neighbor is an assertive, aggressive, extremely effective businessman. This burglary, this violation, was felt by him as a real threat to his masculinity. Accustomed to warding off passivity with aggression, he elaborated fantasies in which he pierced the oppenent.

The individual's personality will determine the degree of impact and the nature of the response to traumatic events. The greater the fear of passivity, the greater the effect of mugging, burglary, and other such violent crimes. It is important to note that some persons are pathologically unconflicted about passivity. One patient enjoyed various acts of "courage" and he had relished death-defying war experiences. He frequently shut off the motor when flying his plane and used it as a glider. This same patient was remarkably and genuinely unafraid of a gangster with whom he became involved. Passive in many respects, he was bisexual and his lack of "masculine protest" or macho spirit may have been responsible for the fact that passivity posed almost no threat to him.

Issues of self-esteem are much more likely to appear in men involved in such violent crimes than in women. Culturally, men are still expected to be strong, to fight and defend themselves. If a man fails to do so when attacked, as is likely and often wise, he is prone to suffer some depreciation of his self-image. Being vulnerable is usually less threatening to a female in terms of issues of self-esteem.

Finally, "bystanders" to violence are often emotionally affected and their problems ought to be considered equally seriously. A patient's roommate was murdered in the apartment they shared: The patient actually found the girl dead. She was very disorganized by the experience, and the upset spread through her entire family. All the therapist can do in such a tragic instance is help the patient work through the experience in terms of his or her own personal psychodynamics, history, and general life situation.

As in the case of sexual assaults, it is often a delicate procedure to explore possible invitations, conscious or unconscious, to crime against the person and property. The therapist must work with the defective judgement and whatever factors involving unconscious motivation contribute to it. In other instances, the specific meaning of any violence to a given person, in the light of his personal history, has to be analyzed.

8. Specific Responses to Rape

Rape is now seen primarily as a crime of violence, not primarily an act of a sexual nature. The women's liberation movement has been responsible for this broader understanding of rape. It has become clear that provocativeness on the part of the woman does not usually play a role; most rapists attack the first woman coming their way, apparently almost independent of age or of looks. On the other hand, the prevailing spirit of women's liberation makes it most difficult to discuss the fact that in some social situations where the rape victim is not simply assaulted in a dark park, unconscious seductiveness on the part of the woman or poor judgement, possibly combined with unconscious impulses, may still play a role.

When it appears that the woman may have been seductive, it is very important to explore the specific psychodynamics. As with all major contemporary events, the impact of the experience has to be seen in relation to the patient's total personality and life history, and common denominators should be established and worked through. Special attention must be paid to masochistic character features and inappropriate guilt feelings related to possible masochistic enjoyment of the violence. Previously existing rape fantasies especially must be explored.

Generally, rape will induce feelings of violation, feelings of helplessness and panic in direct relation to the individual history. Early childhood situations — seduction, forced sex play, primal scenes — will be reawakened with marked intensity.

The Rape Victim, by Elaine Hilberman (29), explores the socio-cultural context of rape and delineates advances made in helping the rape victim. Reactions to rape are grouped into four phases:

1) *An anticipatory or "threat" phase* describes the fine balance between the need to protect one's illusion of invulnerability and the awareness of the threatening reality, with some attempt to protect oneself from — and prepare for — the danger.

2) The *impact phase* brings increased vigilance as a defense mechanism, followed by diminished alertness, numbness, dullness, and affective and memory disturbances, and a general disorganization. In rape victims studied, 25 percent appeared unperturbed. Twenty-five percent had paralyzing anxiety, hysteria, and confusion. The remaining majority were simply stunned and bewildered.

3) In the *recoil phase*, there is a return of emotional expression and awareness. It is in this phase that the therapist can be particularly useful in helping the patient reconstitute. Depending on how the patient perceives the events, behaviors, and feelings, there will either be a sharp decrease in self-esteem and self-confidence with attendant psychodynamic sequelae, or an adaptive increase in these factors.

4) In the *post-traumatic phase*, the patient has maximally reconstituted and can recall the event, repairing whatever temporary damage was done.

Unresolved, unworked-through sequaelae of rape may present as symptoms like claustrophobia, social withdrawal, anxiety attacks, nightmares, and rages loosely focused around issues of helplessness and violation.

Supporting the patient in deciding whether to tell the family, the husband or lover, friends or children, and in assessing the implications of not doing so, is an important task for the therapist. For instance, a woman whose "macho" husband was very likely to hold the rape against her, and to see her as devalued, felt unable to tell him about this act of violence. She then acted out violently at her workplace, where the events occurred. She was painfully conflicted in a realistically difficult situation. Concerns about newspaper publicity, community gossip, social and professional ostracism need to be realistically and supportively addressed. Possible pregnancy, venereal disease, the question of legal prosecution of the rapist and dangers of vengeance for reporting the rape are fears that routinely appear and should be explored and resolved.

9. Specific Responses to Accidents

Accidents are often forms of acting out. It is believed, for instance, that many automobile accidents are suicides or suicide attempts. The therapist must thoroughly explore all the details surrounding the "accident," including especially the patient's thought content and preoccupations before, during, and after the event. Fantasies and dreams will also be helpful in making the assessment.

In order to avoid phenomena akin to traumatic neuroses, to avoid lingering after-effects, denial must be staunchly interpreted. As in pathological mourning or the absence of mourning, the therapist must help the patient do the working through. As mentioned before, Lindemann (37) found in his classic study of the Boston Coconut Grove fire that surviving victims and relatives show a high incidence of psychosomatic disorders and strictly psychological/psychiatric disorders if working through and mourning work of the experience is not accomplished. Victims of violent crimes and experiences suffer similarly and an adequate and thorough working through is crucial. At times an accident will precipitate the reemergence of childhood anxieties, resulting in fears of helplessness and passivity, fears of castration, or fear of poor impulse control. As usual, the therapist's main task is to find the common denominators between the precipitating event and the historical situations in the patient's life, in order to help him understand and deal with his trauma.

10. Specific Responses to the Threat of Ecological Catastrophy

It is one of the earmarks of our decade that the threat of ecological catastrophies looms over us, carrying with it the threat of immediate death or long-lingering moribundity. The fear of nuclear accidents from nuclear plants such as the Three-Mile Island one is an ever-present source of anxiety. The possibility of nuclear accidents or even nuclear war has been called the final epidemic.

This fear of a nuclear holocaust has affected an entire generation. Such phrases as "Have a good day," or "Take care," or "Take one day at a time," are linguistic reflections of this concern.

At times, actual panics have broken out, such as in instances of malfunctioning controls in the nuclear reactors. Some have had to live with other threats to their lives, such as the wide-spread dioxin contamination. Whole towns evidenced panic and had to be evacuated to avoid physical harm. In 1983, in one school in Yonkers, New York, it was discovered that asbestos was flaking off the ceilings. Asbestos, in the past, was considered a valuable protection against the outbreak of fire, but in recent years, it has been shown to cause lung disease and in the long run, possibly lung cancer. Parents and students were frantic and turblent meetings were held. These examples could be multiplied manifold.

It is therefore extremely likely that an ever increasing number of patients will be turning up in clinics and private offices with panic reactions of one kind or another, a direct response to ecological threats. As in all catastrophic situations, the chances are that fearful fantasies will outrun even the stark realities. It will be important to help not only with realistic reassurances, but also to reduce the irrational fantasies that complicate the ability to cope with reality.

In these instances, Brief Intensive Group Psychotherapy, with numbers of people afflicted, may be the method of choice.

VIII.
The Intensive
BRIEF AND EMERGENCY PSYCHOTHERAPY
(B.E.P.)
of
PHOBIAS (and ANXIETY HYSTERIAS)

VIII. PHOBIAS (and ANXIETY HYSTERIAS)

THEORETICAL CONSIDERATIONS

Anxiety hysterias and phobias are dynamically and phenomenologically closely related (24). They are also frequently interrelated and coexistent in the same person. Hypochondriacal symptoms, for instance, as a form of anxiety hysteria, often lead to phobic avoidance of conditions which are seen as possibly leading to the feared illness. Therefore, I will discuss these two conditions interchangeably.

Phobias are frequently longstanding problems, *but at times approach emergency conditions*: For example, the business executive who is slated to fly to a conference in Europe and develops an acute fear of flying; the plight of a salesman in Manhattan who suddenly panics at the prospect of riding an elevator; the sudden fear of entering a subway which makes it impossible for a New York secretary to hold her job.

I once treated an academician who developed a sudden panic about the prospect of delivering a paper before a peer group, and a college student who was headed for academic disaster because of acute examination anxiety. Another patient, a housewife, was virtually incapacitated because of an agoraphobia which interfered with her shopping and a businessman was unable to drive from his home to his business 18 miles away because of his phobia about driving a car.

Some general propositions hold true for all phobias: The fear has to involve a feared drive. It may be an aggressive drive, as in the case of the fear of driving: all the horsepower might get out of hand and kill somebody. Or there may be a variety of sexual fears involved: The fear of driving may involve the fantasy of feeling faint and of having to pull over to the side of the road. One man was afraid that when this happened a state trooper would have to come to his aid and put him in an ambulance, an expression of fears of passivity and also latent homosexuality. Similarly, a woman may fear that once she is on the side of the road, she will be helpless and at the mercy of any aggressor, even someone who might sexually molest her.

The agoraphobic housewife was able to navigate the streets when she was in low heels and shabby clothes, but not when she was wearing high heels and was fashionably dressed: in the latter instance, her fear was that she might be unsteady on her feet, fall and expose herself.

The salesman who feared riding an elevator was experiencing a kind of claustrophobia, related to his fear of being overwhelmed or smothered, obviously suffering the sequaelae of what Phillip Wylie termed "smotherhood." Others may have different components to their elevator or subway anxieties, and the fear of flying hardly fits a set formula.

TEN SPECIFIC FACTORS IN THE
THERAPEUTIC MANAGEMENT
OF PHOBIAS

1. SPECIFIC DYNAMICS OF THE DIFFERENT PHOBIAS

2. SPECIFIC PHOBIAS AS PART OF A FAMILY AND
   CULTURAL CONTEXT

3. OVERDETERMINED INDIVIDUAL PATHOGENESIS OF
   PHOBIAS

4. ASK THE PATIENT TO FACE THE PHOBIC SITUATION
   AND REPORT BACK

5. WORK THROUGH INSIGHTS OBTAINED IN THE ACTUAL
   PHOBIC SITUATION

6. DRUGS FOR SYMPTOMATIC RELIEF OF SOME PHOBIAS

7. COUNTER-PHOBIC SYMBOLS AND DEFENSES

8. MIGRATORY PHOBIAS

9. PAN-PHOBIAS

10. SOMATIC DELUSIONS

1. Specific Dynamics of the Different Phobias

As to specific phobias, *agoraphobia* is possibly the most frequently encountered one. It may take the form of not being able to cross streets, not being able to travel any distance from home, not being able to go out of the house at all without being accompanied by a person who serves the function of a counter-phobic symbol. In agoraphobics, one will frequently elicit an earlier history of *school phobias*, which serves to highlight the fact that separation/individuation and fear of loss of the love object, usually the mother, play a marked role in the personality constellation.

Classically, we believe that fear of regressive impulses makes it difficult to leave mother lest she be the victim of one's death wishes — while one isn't looking. Thus, in history taking, exploring ambivalence toward the maternal figure is especially important.

It is fascinating that very often only travelling *away* from home is anxiety-arousing for agoraphobic patients. Once they are on the return trip, they are perfectly comfortable.

In female patients especially, problems of *exhibitionism* often play a marked role in the agoraphobia. As indicated, a primary fear is often that the person will faint on the street; if one explores a little further, what is usually elicited is that she fears that her skirt may ride up or that a man may pick her up from the street and take sexual advantage of her.

With regard to the fear of separation, agoraphobs often can manage when accompanied by a counterphobic figure. I treated an elderly woman who could manage the streets and go to the supermarket if she was pushing around an empty baby carriage. Apparently, just the idea of holding on to something (in this case, something representative of a child) made it possible for her to navigate.

Passivity and fear/desire of passivity play a role in both males and females. It may involve a number of variations on the theme of helplessness, which they fear as much as they crave the dependence.

The fear of driving often involves all the components of an agoraphobia but in addition has dominantly a fear of aggression: all the horsepower at one's command produce fantasies of crashing into somebody. The outstanding phenomenon may be more generally a fear of loss of control under these circumstances.

Claustrophobia occurs frequently, and is sometimes associated with an agoraphobia. In a nutshell, Philip Wiley's idea of "smotherhood" conveys the most frequent etiology of claustrophobia — a feeling of being too controlled, held too tightly, being unable to breathe; it is most often directly related to having felt that way earlier in one's life, toward the maternal figure especially.

Elevator phobias and fears of flying often contain elements of claustrophobia, namely being enclosed and unable to get out; similar dynamics hold true for subway anxieties. As to further specific factors, the fear of flying involves the general fear of helplessness, possibly crashing, i.e., falling, thus completely passive. For some, the feeling of rising into the air has sexual significance akin to erection and that will cause anxiety. In *elevator phobias* the very closeness to people may produce sexual fears, in addition to claustrophobic anxieties. The stimulation associated with the feeling of rising may unconsciously produce sexual fears, especially in adolescents. As a matter of fact, the fear of riding a railroad, to the extent that people still do so, is also most often related to sexual stimulation induced by the rhythmical movement of the train. This may also hold true in a subway phobia, though the claustrophobic aspects are usually the most readily complained about.

2. Specific Phobias as Part of a Family and Cultural Context

Aside from the individual dynamics, many phobias are acquired by "contagion": They may run in families and *specific phobias may have to be understood as part of a family context*. Certain cultural conditions may also have to be taken into consideration. For example, in some ethnic groups remaining close to the home and to the nuclear family is a basic pattern, and it is sometimes difficult to draw the line between what is normal for them culturally and what should be considered a pathological phobia, except when the patient complains about the fear as being ego alien.

In some instances, the phobic behavior may be acquired by identification with a parental figure: a mother's fear of death or illness, or of leaving the home for long periods, may be duplicated in her offspring.

3. Individual Overdetermined Pathogenesis of Phobias

Though there are some general propositions which hold true for most phobias, and some propositions which hold true for specific phobias, there are, of course, *individual aspects to every phobic reaction*, which hold true for each individual patient and not for others.

Studying the *onset* of the phobia (or anxiety hysteria) will usually most clearly reveal the individual features. The more specifically one establishes the *onset*, the more insight one gets into the specific meaning. The executive who suddenly developed a fear of flying to Europe had flown frequently before. But this trip involved going to Paris and he viewed Paris as a dangerously beckoning sin city. His fear then was only tangentially related to flying per se.

A gas mechanic developed a fear of dying of a heart attack one Saturday morning at 10:30 A.M. (some might consider his condition an anxiety hysteria rather than a phobia) and rushed to the medical emergency clinic where he was examined and found to be perfectly healthy. It took a good deal of work to establish the circumstances of his reaction. He related to me that, just prior to his heart palpitations, a tank car had delivered gasoline to the station where he worked. I at first wondered whether his anxiety was by chance related to a fear of explosion. This hypothesis was not substantiated. It then turned out that his boss was away on vacation and he had been left in charge of the gas station; I wondered whether he feared some recriminations upon the boss' return or whether he had by chance some fantasies of replacing the boss, which made him feel guilty and anxious. These hypotheses were also not substantiated.

Upon further delving, I finally began to understand the relevant dynamics. It emerged that a friend of his had come by and had teased him. The patient had just given some blood for this man's sick aunt and so had a few other people. But this particular friend had apparently been turned away by the hospital for one reason or another. The patient suddenly felt greatly taken advantage of, and this feeling coalesced with a recent situation in which he felt taken advantage of by his former wife, whom he was supporting. At this occasion, powerful wishes to be taken care of were revived from a childhood which had shared deprivation and overindulgence by the mother. In his case, then, the anxiety hysteria was related to the wish for passivity as well as his profound oral rage. This rage probably precipitated the palpitations, which he interpreted as a cardiac illness. As it turned out, the patient also suffered from a dynamically closely related agoraphobia, which kept him dependent.

A woman patient had an acute fear of flying, which had developed just prior to her having to leave on a lengthy European vacation. Upon closer examination, it was neither the fear of passivity nor a variety of claustrophobia, but a quite unique constellation that disturbed her. She had no fear of flying over various parts of the country on the way to Europe; the one part of the flight that she did dread was going from Barcelona to Madrid and then to North Africa. What she really feared was that if the plan crashed over the high mountainous plateau of Spain, she would then face a painful death by starvation or lack of water. This absurd fear emerged only after painstaking investigation. She was obviously intelligent enough to realize that if the plane really did crash, she would be dead on impact and certainly never have to face her particular fears.

Another patient with a fear of flying was typically only afraid of flying over the ocean. As irrational as the above patient, he dreaded the idea of being devoured by sharks, dead or alive, and this was what really deterred him from flying.

While the above are extreme examples of the specificity of irrational and often unconscious fears, I hope that they indicate the need for going beyond exploration of the general formula in the phobic reaction.

4. Ask the Patient to Face the Phobic Situation and Report Back

Some general considerations: In all instances, after an initial exploration of the dynamics of the problem, *the patient has to be asked to face the phobic situation and then report back on the discomfort, which furnishes further material for understanding.*

It is only too easy in all of psychotherapy to have the patient understand the problem intellectually. It is also essential that the patient dare approach the anxiety-arousing situation while in treatment. It is not easy technically to decide when best to ask the patient to face the feared situation, be it subway or elevator — which is easier than an international flight. I would suggest the following guideline: Whenever the basics have been worked through, one should have the patient expose himself to the possible minimum: e.g., ride one station on the subway; ride the elevator for one or two floors. He should then report back how he felt — whatever emotion went with the experience will then provide new material for the working through.

Aside from the conceptual working through, this situation has elements of desensitization in terms of conditioning theory. Slowly the patient should be encouraged and can be expected to bear more anxiety, as well as bring material which will further decrease the anxiety. It is one of the many areas where a psychoanalytic approach and a behavioral approach overlap.

5. Work Through Insights Obtained in the Actual Phobic Situation

Working through of insights attained in the actual phobic situation is extremely important and related to the idea of reconditioning. Earlier, I discussed working through as a general part of the therapeutic process (See Page 41): the application of insight to a variety of situations including everyday life as well as the transference situation.

What has been said there generally holds true specifically for phobic conditions. Every insight acquired cognitively has to be applied in the phobic situation. There must be a steady interchange between the process of learning by insight and the process of learning by conditioning, in order to attain optimal therapeutic results.

6. Drugs for Symptomatic Relief of Some Phobias

Drugs, especially energizers and anti-depressants, have been found useful in the symptomatic relief of some phobias. These may prove extremely helpful in instances where phobias interfere with important daily functioning, including being able to perform one's job. It is unlikely that the drugs do more than afford symptomatic relief, until psychotherapy can take effect. Nevertheless, I would not want to underestimate the usefulness of these drugs, especially when phobias are likely to cause a major disruption in someone's life. There are also some phobic patients who are almost refractory to psychotherapy, brief or long, and in these cases prolonged drug use is sometimes the only possible remedy.

The drug which has been found most useful for phobias and obsessions is chlorimipramine (Anafranil), a drug which is used in most of the world but which is not, as yet, approved by the FDA in the United States.

When, for some reason, tricyclic drugs are not effective or for some other reason contraindicated, anxiolitic drugs may prove useful in the temporary or long-term management of phobias.

Patients with agoraphobia who do not have someone available to accompany them to the office may, with the help of drugs, at least be able to come for psychotherapy. The drugs, in this instance, serve as the enabling conditions for psychotherapy.

7. Counter-Phobic Symbols and Defenses

A phobic patient may, at first, have to be accompanied to the office by a person functioning as a counter-phobic protection, until drugs or interpretation make this unnecessary. It is part of widespread superstition that a coin, medal, rabbit's foot or some other object may protect one against everything from accidents to the evil eye. The counterphobic symbol serves in the same capacity, be it a person or an object.

The gas station attendant mentioned earlier carried with him a small book of inspirational nature. When he felt anxious, he looked for some inspiring paragraph full of moral or other exhortations. With the book right next to him, he was able to drive and attend to his other daily activities.

8. "Migratory" Phobias

Some phobic patients suffer, at first, from free-floating anxiety attacks and usually, after some time, this anxiety is "bound, " in the form of an anxiety hysteria or sometimes in the form of a phobia. At other times, the anxiety will resolve itself into a depression. The fact is that one must remember that all symptoms are *attempts at coping*: sometimes one symptom and sometimes another copes with the basic anxiety. In the most disturbed people, a paranoid system is the coping device they eventually arrive at to bind their anxiety.

The same holds true for phobias. To a certain extent, the more limited the phobia, the relatively less intrusive it is in a person's lifestyle. The more generalized the phobia, the more crippling it is. Some people do not manage to arrive at one optimal configuration of forces of fears and defenses against them, and therefore have frequently changing anxiety hysterias or phobias, in the form of migratory phobias.

Outstanding among these are hypochondriacal concerns. Some patients are especially frustrating to their internists because they arrive one day gravely concerned about a brain tumor, and two days later upset over a supposedly impending heart attack. As soon as they are reassured about these anxieties, they may develop a preoccupation with a rectal cancer or leukemia. I have tended to speak of these fears as "migratory phobias." Having analyzed many patients at length, I have found that these fears can usually be reduced to an underlying castration fear, which unconsciously is ascribed to one part of the body after another. The fact is that one has to deal with the basic anxiety, which then automatically interferes wih the constantly changing pattern of baffling preoccupations with bodily illness.

In this context, "castration anxiety" should not be taken too literally. What it really relates to usually is some vague childhood anxiety of being harmed. It need not refer to a specific loss of the penis or, as castration would be more properly related to, of the testicles. It can also, in women, just carry the implication of somehow being hurt. This is often the result of having overheard the parents in sexual relations, the primal scene, and somehow developing some vague anxiety of something dreadful and painful being done to one.

9. Pan-Phobias

Pan-phobias may look like migratory phobias, except for the fact that the patient, at the same time, is afraid of many different things. There may be a fear of illness by touching supposedly contaminated objects along with a fear of falling bricks. A claustrophobia may exist alongside an agoraphobia, etc. The prototypical case of the billionaire Howard Hughes serves as a concrete and publicly known example. Eventually he is believed to have insisted on wearing cotton gloves, eating only the simplest of food, and surrounded himself with myriad protections against illness, germs or other contamination. Obsessions and phobias, then, easily go hand in hand. It has been suggested that such conditions merit being considered "schizophrenia," or what had once been described as "psudoneurotic schizophrenia." These days, such patients are often referred to as suffering from a borderline condition. Except for some effect on isolated aspects of the dysfunction, brief therapy and, for that matter, long-term therapy, stand only a poor chance of making a difference, and then only by dealing with the complex and very primitive basic dynamics.

10. Somatic Delusions

Somatic delusions, like pan-phobias, also belong to the most baffling, bizarre and therapeutically frustrating conditions. It is important not to mistake them for a mere phobia or an anxiety hysteria. This happens all too frequently, to the misfortune of both patient and therapist.

125

One suffering patient complained of troublesome constipation and with it, cramps in her abdomen. She took an inordinate amount of laxatives but always felt that she had not entirely relieved herself. She went from internist to internist, aside from numerous psychiatric consultations. The thought of not having had enough of a bowel movement obsessed her all day. She would see people on T.V. and think that they were lucky; they obviously looked happy because they had just had a satisfying bowel movement. If she met people on the street, she would be preoccupied with the same thought. Painstaking anamnesis and exploration made it clear that, at least unconsciously (and not *quite* so unconsciously), she believed she had some growth or organism living within her intestines, and that that was what she was trying to rid herself of. Analytically speaking, this was a symbol for a primitive fantasy of impregnation, but a fetus which was identified with an aggressive devouring character, which she translated at times into a concern about a malignancy. Long drawn out treatment was quite unsuccessful. After having been refused by at least half a dozen surgeons, she finally found one who operated on her and removed a large amount of intestine. A few weeks after the surgery, it was he who called me in desperation. The patient had returned to her preoccupation with her bowels and her bowel movements.

Another patient was tortured by the fear of being afflicted with rabies. He was constantly washing his hands and going from one doctor to another for reassurance that he did not, in fact, have rabies.

A man was troubled by the feeling that his tongue was too big for his mouth, and he felt uncomfortable with his mouth either open or closed.

Another patient had the preoccupation that his shoes were too tight and/ or too loose. He eventually was unable to perform any work. As soon as he would tighten his shoelaces, he would promptly feel that they were too tight. Upon opening them, he would be troubled by the feeling that they were far too loose. Chances are that in this case, the feet had some phallic significance, just as the tongue of the other patient did, and that these patients were preoccupied with concerns of a superficially phallic but also pre-genital nature.

As might be surmised, psychotherapy was not at all successful with these patients, who are sometimes said to be suffering from a mono-symptomatic delusion. All of these patients apparently had no other hallucinations or delusions, and aside from the particular somatic delusions, their reality testing was intact.

I am mentioning this condition in this context only to make clear that unfortunately, in my experience, psychotherapy of short or long term nature has virtually nothing to offer such patients. However, there is a report that a drug called Pimozide may be effective in treating these otherwise refractory conditions. This is suggested by Alistair Munro, M.D. (55), who speaks of these conditions as "Monosymptomatic Hypochondriacal Psychosis (MHP)", My observations concur with his in that he also speaks of a *single* hypochondriacal delusion. He suggests a single morning dose of Pimozide, ranging between 2 and 12 mg.

IX.
The Intensive
BRIEF AND EMERGENCY PSYCHOTHERAPY
(B. E. P.)
of
PANIC

IX. PANIC

THEORETICAL CONSIDERATIONS

Panic may occur in the patient in several different forms. The three main types are: endogenous, exogenous, and mixed panics.

1. The Endogenous Panic:

This state is characterized by a complaint of a feeling of dread, which usually involves somatic manifestations such as difficulties in breathing, heart palpitations, flushed skin: There is a fear of something awful happening, such as impending death, disaster, or "going crazy." It is akin to free-floating anxiety, only much more severe. In all instances, the cause of the panic or anxiety is *unknown* to the patient. This condition occurs frequently in incipient psychoses, but may also occur in non-psychotic individuals, with an extreme intensity.

2. The Exogenous Panic:

This state is precipitated by an external event, such as rape, mugging, accident, etc.

3. The "Mixed" Panic:

This is a term I use to refer to panics induced by street drugs, specifically. Occasionally, it may also occur with the use of prescription drugs. I speak of it as "mixed" because we know, on the one hand, that the drug has caused it; on the other hand, the drug provides for the emergence of fantasies which are unique to the patient's personality. These fantasies or feelings are therefore both endogenous and exogenous, and in turn are what frightens the patient. Consequently, one has to deal both with the toxic and the psychodynamic conditions. Of course, we may also be dealing with flashbacks, where no drug was taken recently, but some external condition has precipitated the panic-arousing effect that past intake of drugs had caused. The potentially disturbing aspects of marijuana, LSD, Speed, Angel Dust, and cocaine are well known. Even some over-the-counter drugs may induce palpitations, which some people interpret as anxiety. In fact, quite paradoxically, some people will react to any sedative with anxiety. Essentially, this occurs because they sense a loss of control and estrangement.

TEN SPECIFIC FACTORS IN THE THERAPEUTIC MANAGEMENT OF PANIC

1. ESTABLISH THE UNCONSCIOUS CAUSE OF THE ENDOGENOUS PANIC

2. CONTINUITY BETWEEN IMMEDIATE PANIC, PRECIPITATING FACTORS AND LIFE HISTORY

3. INTELLECTUAL EXPLANATION AS PART OF ESTABLISHING CONTINUITY

4. EXOGENOUS PANIC: UNCONSCIOUS MEANING OF EXTERNAL EVENT

5. RELATE EXOGENOUS PANIC TO ENDOGENOUS FACTORS, MAKING IT EGO ALIEN

6. ENDOGENOUS PANIC AS PART OF AN INCIPIENT PSYCHOSIS

7. BE COMPLETELY AVAILABLE TO PATIENT

8. PROVIDE A STRUCTURE

9. INTERPRET DENIAL

10. USE CATHARSIS OR MEDIATE CATHARSIS

1. Establish the Unconscious Cause of the Endogenous Panic

There are a number of dynamic patterns which are the principal causes of endogenous panic :

1. *Fear of loss of impulse control,* whether of an aggressive or sexual nature.

2. *Anniversary reactions* most often manifest themselves as a depression, but sometimes present as panics and psychotic states. There is excellent statistical evidence that a significant number of people enter a psychiatric hospital on an anniversary date.

3. *Separation anxiety,* especially in the individual who needs symbiotic relationships.

4. *Drugs,* such as marijuana, LSD, or amphetamines, may induce altered states of mind, flashbacks, and consequent acute panic states. Ocassionally, a drug such as the phenothiazines will induce panic as a paradoxical reaction. Such feelings of loss of control due to the felt effect of the drug also sometimes occur with the fast-acting barbiturates.

5. *Severe superego reactions* in response to increased sexual or aggressive feelings and behaviors. This may take various forms, such as the fear of pregnancy, the fear of venereal disease, or a free-floating panic without manifest content.

6. *Moral masochism,* of which a success neuroris is one aspect. Any new attainment, including therapeutic progress, takes on a forbidden oedipal meaning which is then responded to with panic. This may happen to people who have made a major advance or any marked improvement in any area in their lives. If it occurs in response to therapeutic progress, it is called a "negative therapeutic response."

7. *A sudden decrease in self-esteem.* In the long run this may lead to a depression and, under certain circumstances, a manic disorder. The first phenomenon at the onset of a psychosis may be a panic. Some neurotic people, on the other hand, have frequent panics that are *not* transitional phenomena to a more severe disorder.

8. *Depersonalization* is usually an outgrowth of unacceptable feelings of aggression of one part of the self against another part of the self. Jacobson (31) points out that if the aggression emanates from the superego and is directed toward the self, the patient will suffer primarily from feelings of guilt.

9. *Derealization,* even in such mild forms as déjà vu, may also produce secondary panic by the very nature of the subjective experience.

10. Severely *traumatic events* may produce panic.

2. Continuity Between Immediate Panic, Precipitating Factors and Life History

It is essential to demonstrate clearly to the patient a continuity between the immediate panic, the precipitating factors and the life history. This gives the patient at least some feeling of control over what seems frighteningly ego-alien.

In my own practice, the assassination of President Kennedy touched off panic reactions in three patients, all of whom were overwhelmed with a sense of impending disaster. With one, there was identification with the assassin; this man feared the outbreak of his own aggressive drives. After a period of sexual abstinence he had been looking forward to spending the night with a woman but now hesitated. With another patient the central idea was: "If a man as powerful as Kennedy can be killed, what will happen to a simple "shnook" like me?" The third patient experienced the loss of President Kennedy with a remembrance of the death of her mother during the patient's childhood which had left her feeling unprotected and helpless.

The features of the exogenous circumstances and the form and content of the panic must be linked in interpretation to the patient's specific dynamics and genetic antecedents. Thus the patient who identified with President Kennedy's assassin was reminded of the event in his childhood when he was four years old and his father struck his mother during a quarrel.

3. Intellectual Explanation as Part of Establishing Continuity

A purely intellectual explanation and understanding are generally not highly thought of as tools of dynamic psychotherapy. In the case of a panic, however, the discontinuity of experience is responsible for much of the disturbance; thus even an intellectual understanding, by helping the patient to see the continuity, usually has a reassuring effect on the patient: He feels "less crazy."

4. Exogenous Panic: Unconscious Meaning of External Event

The main aspect to keep in mind in an exogenous panic is that it is essential to understand the *unconscious meaning that the external event holds for a particular patient.* This point has been discussed previously in this book with regard to other external events, such as physical illness, mugging, etc., and holds true especially in this regard.

The exogenous panic, to a large extent, derives its emotional charge from the unconscious meaning it has for the patient. One young man, for example, found his car broken into and vandalized; the panic he experienced was related to his identifying with the car. He felt that he might similarly be the victim of this type of assault at any time.

5. Convert Exogenous Panic to Endogenous, Making it Ego Alien

The therapist can employ certain techniques to help make the panic ego alien. He may say, "Yes, this is a terrible situation. But, I believe, if we asked ten people who have had similar experiences, they would most likely react quite differently from you." By this means the therapist can drive a wedge between the patient's strictly subjective experience of panic and other responses and introduce some perspective. This distancing also aids the process of converting the panic from being exogenous to an awareness of its subjective aspects. The endogenous factor, the unconscious conflict or impulse causing irrational anxiety or panic, will have a disorganizing effect on the patient's mental functioning in proportion to the brittleness of the patient's premorbid personality.

In summary, with an exogenous panic, part of the therapist's main task is to immediately make the experience ego alien by emphasizing that others have had similar experiences with less resulting anxiety, and to explore the patient's particular reaction in the context of the specific panic-inducing situation and in the broader context of his personal history, preexisting conflicts and idiosyncratic set of apperceptive distortions.

The young man who responded with a panic to the damage to his car has to realize that what frightens him is not the danger of living in New York City, but rather his general fears of passivity and castration.

6. Endogenous Panic as Part of an Incipient Psychosis

In the case of endogenous panic as part of an incipient psychosis, the unconscious, not quite perceived, cause of the patient's distress is his fear of the primary process breaking through and critically impairing reality testing and judgment. Also contributing to the panic is the fear of possible loss of drive control: "I might just start to jump up and down and yell or hit people."

The primary therapeutic maneuver will be to show the patient continuity between his fear and the precipitating circumstances or experiences. This should have a quieting effect, helping him to feel that he is, after all, not "losing his grip."

7. Be Completely Available to the Patient

The first rule that the therapist must follow in a panic situation is to make himself completely available to the patient. Since the patient feels totally helpless, as defenseless as a small child, he must be made to feel that the therapist is there for him to reach out to.

If the patient calls in the middle of the night in a panic, the therapist should simply listen for a time, until he ascertains the nature of the panic. He must understand the exact nature of the patient's physical surroundings and availability of others: Is he in a strange place? A public place? Is he in bed at home with the lights on? Is there someone with him or someone in close proximity? A friend who can be called? etc. Having ascertained these essentials, the therapist can then engage in some intervention. Talking with the patient over the phone, he can offer support and sometimes insight.

Being alone will increase the patient's panic; the therapist should urge him to stay with another person for a while. The patient should be asked to call the therapist again, after he has called in another member of the household or has arrived at the home of a friend or relative. This show of interest and concern on the therapist's part will help the patient enormously. The intervention must be followed up by an appointment to see the patient at the earliest possible date.

8. Provide a Structure

In a panic situation, almost any structure the therapist can provide is helpful. The first bombings of London during World War II caused emotional havoc. After some very definite rules were established for behavior during bombings, civilian panics virtually disappeared. Furthermore, if adults were panicky during the blitz, children were also. But if the parents remained calm with a definite procedure to follow, the children were also.

Similarly, a patient should be helped to increase signal awareness. Being able to pick up clues that he is beginning to experience anxiety helps him anticipate and avoid a total panic.

When a patient comes to a first session in a panic, the therapist should, as in all crisis situations, deal with the most immediate concerns. He should get to know the patient, obtain a data base which includes the chief complaint, any related complaints, life history, and the precipitating factors related to his current panic, as well as the reason for the patient's decision to seek help now. He should review the nature of the panic for the patient, establishing continuity between the patient's present fears and his past experiences, giving the patient a feeling of control over the panic, assuring him that it *can be handled, that it has causal connections,* and need not be experienced as an alien force, as something beyond his power to understand and work through.

9. Interpret Denial

The therapist must be alert to the operation of denial and repression and actively interfere with these when they are excessive, pointing out to the patient that his panics always arise when a stimulus or excitation is denied or repressed.

10. Use of Catharsis or Mediate Catharsis

Cathartic expression of the affects and ideation associated with the panic should be encouraged. The procedure establishes the therapist as an interested and helpful person, permits him to appraise the dynamic content and form of the fear, and, at the same time, provides discharge of sufficient tension so that the patient will be receptive to further therapeutic intervention.

If a direct invitation to catharsis is inadvisable, because of the fragile nature of the patient's ego, *mediate catharsis* may be advisable, as previously discussed. (See chapter 7).

Footnote: The current craze of viewing anxiety conditions as the result of physical symptoms is so counterproductive that it merits a footnote here. The matter of "prolapsed mitral valve" as a cause for anxiety attacks will serve as the best example. There is no doubt that any condition which causes palpitations may lead to the experience of anxiety. Typically, analysts know that unconscious sexual arousal may lead to palpitations and fast breathing and may be experienced as free-floating anxiety.

Historically, there have been two basic general theories of anxiety: The best known one was Cannon's theory of adrenalin production when faced with a dangerous situation (21). Adrenalin poured out as part of the "fight or flight" reflex, leading to greater coagulatability as well as circulatory changes, etc. The main rival theory was the James-Lange theory (35), which held that the subjective experience of anxiety was the secondary result of physiological changes, such as palpitations, muscle tension, etc. It is on this second approach, the James-Lange theory, that current emphasis on physical aspects of anxiety rests, knowingly or unknowingly.

My own experience with anxiety arousal goes back a long time, to Maranon's experiments with the injection of adrenalin. In some, the adrenalin injection would produce anxiety, in others it would not (40). I am satisfied that the *subjective experience of anxiety occurs*, even after the injection of adrenaline, *only* if someone has another anxiety stimulus, including unconscious ideation, and then translates the experience of palpitations into the Gestalt of "anxiety." People without the previous cognitive experience of anxiety experience the dentist's novacaine-adrenaline mixture as unpleasant palpitations, but do not describe it as anxiety.

Thus, treatment of anxiety with propranolol and other drugs can only affect part of what is the general experience of anxiety — i.e., the physiological symptoms — but one still needs psychodynamic treatment to deal with the entire problem and not only with the somatic stimulus.

For a sophisticated discussion of the interaction of cognitive and biological aspects of anxiety see Kandel, Eric R. From metapsychology to molecular biology: Explorations into the nature of anxiety. *Amer. J. Psychiatry.* 140:1277-1293, 1983.

X. Intensive B. E. P. of
FEELINGS OF UNREALITY OF THE SELF
AND OF THE WORLD

X. FEELINGS OF UNREALITY OF THE SELF
AND OF THE WORLD

THEORETICAL CONSIDERATIONS

The individual in a state of depersonalization feels himself to be changed in contrast with his former state of being. He feels himself to be an observer; in effect, a spectator of himself. He senses a loss or loosening of his own identity. Frequently, the patient feels that he no longer has a self to which he can refer directive forces and behavior. He may feel that parts of his body or of his mind are now alien and strange and do not belong to him. In extreme states he will feel that he no longer has a body or that he is not alive. These feelings may extend to the environment, which will seem equally alien and strange to the patient and which will appear to have losts its features of reality. He may believe that there is no world existing; he experiences derealization (5).

TEN SPECIFIC FACTORS RE: FEELINGS OF UNREALITY OF THE SELF AND OF THE WORLD

1. CO-EXISTENCE OF FEELINGS OF UNREALITY OF THE SELF AND OF THE WORLD

2. A CONTINUUM OF PATHOLOGY

3. STATES OF HEIGHTENED AND CHANGED AWARENESS OF THE SELF OR OF THE BODY

4. AGGRESSIVE, SEXUAL, EXHIBITIONISTIC AND SEPARATION ASPECTS

5. DISTURBANCES OF THE SENSE OF SELF AS INTRA-SYSTEMIC EGO DISTURBANCE

6. ESTRANGEMENT RELATED TO PHYSICAL FACTORS

7. DRUG-INDUCED STATES OF UNREALITY (PRESCRIPTION AND STREET DRUGS)

8. DÉJÀ VU AND DÉJÀ RECONNU PHENOMENA

9. GENERAL THERAPEUTIC CONSIDERATIONS

10. DRUG MANAGEMENT

1. Co-existence of Feelings of Unreality of the Self and of the World

I feel that it is imperative to conceive of depersonalization (and derealization) as a more or less extreme variation of the changes in self-perception and feelings of unreality as similar variants of perception of the world that occur constantly in normal life. These changes may often be on a preconscious level, the degree of consciousness depending upon circumstances and individual variations of introspectiveness. Changes in self-perception are probably always associated with changes in perception of the environment. Viewing depersonalization and feelings of unreality as a special aspect of the general problem of perception we can broaden our understanding of the phenomenon, to see its dynamic and genetic relationship to other variants of perception, and to see it as part of a general theory of personality rather than as a form of psychopathology per se.

Everyday life forces a multitude of varying roles on every individual, with concomitant changes of one's self in relation to the environment and coinciding with changes in self-awareness, self-concept, and self-feeling. These changing roles involve those of peer and subordinate and superior, public figure and parent, buyer and seller, and many others; in fact, in subtle ways our role changes in relationship to every person with whom we deal, and every setting in which we move about. In addition, there are of course the more dramatic changes of role from health to illness, civilian to soldier, free man to prisoner, young man to old man.

Even mild feelings of self-consciousness with their altered self-perception may be accompanied by a perceptual distortion of the individual's perception of the world around him, and reactions or observations. In these instances, depersonalization, feelings of unreality, and projection are inextricably linked as a general perceptual distortion of the self and the enviornment.

2. A Continuum of Pathology

A common example of mild depersonalization, in which the simultaneous change of role as well as change of perception of the self and of the environment is clearly evident, can be seen in stage fright. The affected person feels not only as if someone else is talking or acting and that the voice does not sound like his own, but also that minutes seem like hours and that a few steps are like miles. The perception of self as well as of time and space are altered.

Several definite advantages are gained by seeing depersonalization as a variation on a continuum of self-awareness. The first is that it obviates the tendency to identify depersonalization only with specific psychiatric disorders. One may merely say that more or less severe feelings of depersonalization may occur under certain circumstances and may be related to varyingly severe degrees of pathology. This formulation permits one to make an important point: A patient's history of experience with feelings of depersonalization is, by itself, of no specific diagnostic value. The severity of depersonalization probably relates proportionally to the extent to which the patient also evidences disturbances caused by oral problems and also the extent to which he suffers disturbances of the ego boundaries. These, in turn, relate more or less directly to the severity of the neurosis or psychosis.

A second advantage to be gained by considering depersonalization as a general perceptual phenomenon is that it removes the tendency to define it too narrowly as a specific psychic process or even simply as a defense.

A third advantage is that we are enabled to see the many pathways that lead to his phenomenon. Feelings of depersonalization may be produced by a wide variety of drugs, particularly by the psychotomimetics (such as d-lysergic acid diethylamide [LSD] and others). As noted earlier, they may also be caused by simple physiological mechanisms. In a very anxious person with rigid neck muscles there may be sufficient disturbance of proprioception from the nuchal rigidity, with consequent dizziness and disorientation, to account for a feeling of estrangement. A patient who hyperventilates may have a feeling of light-headedness with paresthesia and other sensory peculiarities arising from alkalosis. There may be sufficient muscle spasticity to effect a change in proprioception. These changes may lead to a change in self-perception and to feelings of depersonalization. Feelings of depersonalization associated with dizziness may be produced by nonfocussing of the eyes. Hysterical patients frequently look at near objects as though they were far away. The resulting diplopia and blurring may cause a feeling of unrealness.

Therapeutically, such feelings of depersonalization are often dealt with most effectively by direct means. For example, by interfering with the hyperventilation or alkalosis through the use of muscle relaxants, sedatives or other drugs, one is able to alter the sensory distortions, thereby relieving the distortions in feelings of self-awareness.

Disturbances in the sense of self are also directly related to problems in object relationships: The more primitive the object relationship, the more severe the disturbance of the sense of reality of the self. In severely narcissistic people, the boundary line may almost completely disappear and the person will confuse what is happening to someone else with what is happening to himself: He can become the other person, e.g., a person in a movie.

In primarily symbiotic object relations, a separation may be experienced as a partial loss of the self, with severe anxiety. In primarily anaclitic relations, the feeling of unrealness is most often interrelated with agoraphob symptoms. In primarily ambivalent relationships, agoraphobia is also the most frequently presenting symptom, as if the patient were saying, "I have to be able to see you or how do I know that my hostile wishes haven't killed you?"

The most severe feelings of depersonalization, then, are primarily important in narcissistic and symbiotic relationships. Relief of the acute symptoms is possible in B. E. P., but more profound changes would require long-term treatment.

3. States of Heightened and Changed Awareness of the Self and/or of the Body

Dissociative phenomena may appear in a variety of forms, covering a wide spectrum of experience and behavior. The milder, more common forms often involve a combination of depersonalization and derealization — for example, the feeling of "freaking out," not being "with it," "being on the outside looking in," feeling that "my head is filled with cotton," or "enclosed by a glass wall." Some people (usually hysterics) with relatively mild feelings of derealization actually induce the experience, without knowing they are doing so; for example, if a person looks at an object close up while focusing on the horizon, the pupils become dilated and the close image appears fuzzy, unclear, out of focus. In turn, the fuzziness of the image on the retina induces some feelings of unreality, of being not related to or removed from the environment. Explaining the process to the patient and demonstrating that the symptoms can be produced at will has, at least, a reassuring effect. Dealing with the dynamics of the denial is a more effective measure.

Other patients describe more disturbing phenomena, such as a perception that everything is moving very far away. Objects appear as though they are being viewed through the wrong end of a telescope. The patient feels very strange and/or that the world around him is unreal. He or she may have very disturbing dreams in which figures and objects appear very small. These phenomena can be interpreted as a feeling of a lack of object relations.

Feelings of derealization often occur when people are in a large or strange city. Many people are afraid of New York for this reason. Walking on Wall Street, for example, with its very tall buildings and narrow streets, makes one feel like a figure in a Steig painting. College students often experience these feelings when away from home for the first time, suddenly separated from a familiar small town or country setting and a more structured life. Though they may report anxiety, on closer observation they are actually experiencing feelings of derealization and/or depersonalization. Certainly anxiety itself can set off physiological phenomena, which in turn produces a dissociative experience. Interpreting the feeling of smallness in the first instance, and explaining the physiological process in the latter one, should prove useful.

A classical depersonalization phenomenon is that of having no sense of one's body or body parts. The mouth is most often involved and next the hand. The mouth is the organ obviously most closely associated with passive oral needs, as well as oral aggression, the wish to devour or be devoured. Thus, a numbness of the lips and mouth is a defense or splitting off of dependent passive wishes and/or oral aggression. As the hand is the executive organ for aggression, depersonalizing it or not feeling it is also a way of defending one-self against feelings of aggression by virtually splitting off one part of the self.

Therapeutically, interpretation of the unconscious factors involved is the method of choice.

4. Aggressive, Sexual, Exhibitionistic and Separation Aspects

Depersonalization phenomena most often appear with the emergence of aggressive impulses, separation problems, and less specifically, situations of stimulus hunger or deprivation.

At times of the emergence of powerful aggressive impulses which are dis-approved of and which are then directed against the self, these impulses will set up a situation in which one part of the self looks at another part of the self with disapproving, aggressive connotations. The observing part becomes quite critical of the estranged part. To a certain extent, this is a signal of some alarming condition, very similar to Freud's signal theory of anxiety. Here, the feeling of depersonalization serves as a signal that something is amiss, that there is a strong conflict between some impulse and the superego. This observation of part of the self that is unacceptable can be viewed in terms of Glover's (27) concept of ego nuclei — the different parts of the ego which fuse when personality development proceeds well. When all does not go well, they do not fuse or do not fuse sufficiently, so that under stress the ego nuclei diffuse or dissociate. *Sybil*, a case of multiple personality, is an extreme case in point.

In multiple personality, separate ego states are expressed as though they are complete and different personalities. Under certain circumstances, if these separate ego states (other than the one currently being manifested) are remembered rather than repressed, one ego state may be critical of the other parts, and consequently, the individual will have feelings of estrangement from himself. The splitting of one part of the self from another part of the self and the subsequent disapproval of the one for the other can lead to acting out. Although such extreme splitting is rarely seen, it does indeed exist and in some individuals can lead to major amnesias and/or something akin to multiple personality. It can also be a bridge to acting out, where some un-conscious ego state emerges and takes over in a programmed way. These phenomena are usually due to feelings of aggression. If the person is angry with those around him, these feelings of depersonalization are a way of removing himself from the anger-inducing situation.

Therapeutically, mediate catharsis (see Chapter 7) and interpretation are the most effective means of dealing with the problems discussed above.

Similar disturbances occur when problems of separation appear, because in reality the therapist is unavailable due to illness or vacation, because the patient is going away, or because he has had a significant separation from an important someone in his own world, or is working through early problems of separation. In a dramatic instance of this nature, a patient suddenly developed perioral feelings of depersonalization. He had a very alarming sensation of deadness of the lips and mouth associated with the therapist's leaving for vacation and the threatened separation. He had experienced similar feelings when he went away to college, as well as when he left for school each day as a child. These feelings related to separation from his mother, who had suckled him until he was five.

When suffering from feelings of depersonalization, patients often make urgent attempts to regain some sense of identity and to deal with this disturbing experience. Although psychotics suffer from depersonalization to a greater degree than less severely disturbed patients, nonpsychotics also may exhibit these symptoms and strive to deal with them in various ways. For example, a person may look obsessively into a mirror. When quite disturbed he will wonder if he is seeing his own face; he will grimace and touch the face.

One patient, nowhere near psychotic, dealt with his feeling of depersonalization, with "not being real," by smashing a windowpane with his bare hand. The feeling of being unreal was dispelled by the pain he experienced in smashing the window. Clarence Schulz (50) of Sheppard Pratt Hospital noted that people who have difficulties with depersonalization often touch and slap themselves to increase propriception. Standing in a shower is another way to deal with feelings of unreality and poor body boundaries. Some very disturbed people will spend three or four hours under the shower, comforting themselves with body contact from the water and its feeling of enveloping warmth. These and similar manifestations may, of course, occur in psychotic regressions. Intensive B. E. P. can deal with depersonalization and derealization as acute exacerbations of a chronic process, but not with the chronic process itself.

In striking contrast, some experiences of depersonalization, induced by different means, are often found to be *pleasurable* by many people. Drug states are obvious examples, but depersonalization is also seen in children enjoying the feeling of being dizzy when whirled in the air or riding roller coasters, for example. Intense religious and esthetic experiences may also induce these feelings. "Libidinization of anxiety" occurs when endangering oneself, like hanging from a moving truck or climbing a mountain, becomes a pleasurable form of playing with anxiety. As long as the individual feels he can manage the anxiety through mastery, the ability to tolerate the anxiety is a pleasurable experience.

A similar process takes place when seeing a drama or reading a piece of fiction. The *willing suspension of disbelief* enters in, but at the same time, the individual knows that it is simply the enactment or the telling of a drama. The feelings of unreality remain pleasant provided mastery over them is retained. Many people who purposefully induce feelings of unreality by taking certain drugs, watching a scary movie, etc., can do so in company with pleasurable results. But doing it alone is likely to produce dysphoria and perhaps panic. In fact, any of these self-induced states may get out of hand and create anxiety or panic.

5. Disturbances of the Sense of Self as Intra-Systemic Ego Disturbances

When the self-observing function of the ego is greatly increased, it often produces a feeling of depersonalization. It seems to rob a person of the necessary feeling of "automaticity" of behavior. The patient may complain that he hears everything in his own head before he says it. He feels artificial and removed and devoid of appropriate emotions.

In this state, one part of the self observes the other part of the self, sometimes as a defense against aggression. Clinically, patients then complain of self-consciousness, lack of spontaneity, and an inability to be "with it." They feel the outside looking in, seeing themselves as actors in a play.

Therapeutically, the main task is to help the patient "get in touch" with these split off feelings, thus making them acceptable.

6. Estrangement Related to Physical Factors

Some people react to mariguana or other street drugs, etc., with a panic because they induce feelings of estrangement. It may also be brought about by simple physiological processes, as discussed before.

Therapeutically, medication, "talking down," education, and dealing with unconscious underlying factors is necessary.

7. Drug-Induced States of Unreality (Prescription and Street Drugs)

Many people have dissociative experiences associated with taking a variety of drugs. These induce distortions of the environment, leading to feelings of derealization, and disturbances in body boundaries, leading to experiences of depersonalization. These side-effects of drugs like marijuana and hallucinogens (LSD, or mescaline, for example), are not necessarily limited to the time when the drug is pharmacologically active. "Flashbacks" may occur which cause a return to these disturbing experiences when the patient is otherwise stressed by certain circumstances, including, at times, anxiety-producing periods in psychotherapy itself.

It is less well recognized that some schizophrenics, especially those with awareness of their illness, respond to phenothiazines with a disturbing feeling of being "spaced out."

Many prescription drugs produce a change in proprioceptive feedback. Even diazepam (Valium) by its muscle relaxing effect, may produce proprioceptive changes which secondarily lead to disturbances of the sense of self.

Anti-depressants, and/or energizers, may produce palpitations and, possibly due to hyperventilation, a feeling of lightness of the head, or a feeling of the head being wrapped in cotton — basically, a feeling of depersonalization.

In these instances, proscribing the drug in question, education, and in the case of street drugs, complex treatment programs are indicated.

8. Déjà Vu and Déjà Reconnu Phenomena

The déjà vu phenomena (the feeling of having seen something previously) and déjà reconnu phenomena (the feeling of having experienced something previously) seem to occupy a place somewhere between depersonalization and projection. The experience has an overall quality of strangeness; it seems uncanny, may arouse anxiety, and often makes one feel odd to the point of depersonalization. In this case, external perception may be affected by past fantasies or by congruity with earlier experiences. Interpretation of the connection between contemporary and genetic dynamics is in order. The déjà vu phenomenon may lend itself to an illustration of how nearly everybody may have similar feelings of unreality under certain circumstances — when, for example, modern rapid transportation in a short period of time enables a person to move from one culture or environment to a strange and alien one.

9. General Therapeutic Considerations

Giving the patient some intellectual awareness of the process of depersonalization is generally useful, assuring him that this is not a unique, individual phenomenon, but something that the therapist well understands, that has been met with in many other instances and that can be observed under certain normal circumstances — after waking from a deep sleep or anesthesia, from over-breathing, muscular tension, and perceptual distortions. The effect of the various physiological phenomena may be demonstrated to the patient.

One can demonstrate to the patient that overbreathing will induce an alkalosis, a change of the pH of the blood, which in turn can produce a wide range of phenoena, from tingling in various parts of the body, to spasticity of a variety of muscles, to headaches and tension in the strong muscles of the neck.

If overbreathing plays a frequent role in the induction of depersonalization, the patient may be taught a specific breathing technique: breathing out through a straw or some other small opening with some resistance to exhalation (after free inhalation) while permitting free exhalation in the last moments of exhalation. This will stimulate the Hering-Breuer reflex in the lungs and lead again to an automatically controlled, regular type of breathing which will interfere with the onset of alkalosis and associated depersonalization. The acute states of depersonalization induced by overbreathing and alkalosis can be reversed by the well-known technique of breathing into a paper bag or simply holding one's breath, thereby accumulating more carbon dioxide in the blood stream and reversing the alkalosis and with it the vague feelings associated with depersonalization.

10. Drug Management

Where depersonalization is primarily induced by an anxiety-arousing experience, one can often alleviate the immediate symptoms by drugs such as meprobamate (Miltown, Equanil) and diazepoxide (Librium), etc.

The therapeutic task, even with the help of drugs, is difficult if feelings of depersonalization are related to a need for symbiotic relationships. In such instances, prolonged working through of the dynamic problems is probably necessary.

To the extent to which these problems are dynamically close to those of a depression, anti-depressant drugs may be useful.

APPENDIX

SAMPLE INTERVIEW

Below are a few remarks concerning the process and contents of an initial interview — remarks which highlight a few of the aspects of the patient's functioning and a few technical points. Much more could be said and written; in fact, an entire monograph could be built just upon this interview, but the notes are purposely kept to a bare minimum useful for exemplifying some aspects of the process, rather than offering an exhaustive discussion.

I am grateful to this anonymous man for permitting us to learn from his very moving, human experiences. In the broadest sense, this brief case study shows us that even such horrific life events as front line fighting in Viet Nam and their traumatic impact are best understood in terms of the patient's total personality structure, dynamics and life history.

The interviewee is a 30-year-old Vietnam veteran amputee who was interviewed before an audience of 400 people, as part of a seminar on brief therapy. These circumstances limited some avenues of inquiry. All possible identifying characteristics have been deleted and the interview was videotaped with the patient's permission.

Dr. Bellak: Would you be kind enough and tell me what brought you here in the first place?

Patient: My marriage . . . Me and my wife separated due to problems of mine where I became passive to the point where if she wanted to do something, I just agreed with her to avoid arguments. When I was in Vietnam I had got blown up by a mine. And I did a lot of things in Vietnam that *I don't really like myself for*[1]. And I've just become a mental pacifist because I'm afraid that if *I do get mad, of what I would do*[2], because in Vietnam I had killed at times due to various strenuous circumstances behind it, like having several of my comrades blown away. Being put in a position where I had killed . . . had done things that fell between being justifiable just to stay alive and what is not. And I got to a point where I developed a resistance in myself to the point where *I would not love, would not hate*[3]. And it just got to . . . got to the point where I just could not live in that atmosphere. I had to let out some of the hate or some of the fear. Because I held myself to a point where I did not love. You can't love without hating.

Dr. Bellak: OK. That gives me a bit of an idea. It's my job to ask you questions and try to understand as much as possible. Under the circumstances, if there is something that you don't want to go into, that's your privilege.

All right, you gave me a bit of a general background. Exactly when did you come here. Do you remember the date?

1. This remark indicates intra-aggression.
2. This suggests a fear of loss of impulse control.
3. This represents anhedonia, a result of the patient's repression of anger.

Patient: December 10.

Dr. Bellack: December 10. What was the final push that got you here?

Patient: The final push was that I had been separated from my wife since July before I came here, and from July to December my nerves had gotten to the point where I drank quite a bit. And I'd be sitting at the bar and my hands would be shaking to the point where I couldn't control them. I'd crush a glass just trying to hold them steady. My nerves . . . I was afraid of violence. I was having black-outs. My nerves were catching up with me.

Dr. Bellak: And what would you say made you that nervous? Between July and December especially?

Patient: Not knowing whether I could live with me.

Dr. Bellak: That's too fancy.

Patient: I was trying to make myself not love or hate. Totally blocked it all out. I got to a *point where I had no emotions₃*. Didn't feel.

Dr. Bellak: Where did you live at the time?

Patient: I had an apartment. . .

Dr. Bellak: Did you live by yourself?

Patient: I lived by myself.

Dr. Bellak: Still, there must have been something extra. Something that made you come in here one day in December, after being upset all that while.

Patient: My wife had come in here before and basically she talked me into coming, with the idea that they could give me some better answers.

Dr. Bellak: But was there something extra special that made you come in December and not in July?

Patient: I had got to the point where I had left . . . .by December, I had found out that I could not rationalize some of the things I did by myself. When I was married, I had made myself think that they were rational.

Dr. Bellak: Like?

Patient: Dealing with Nam. I was in several positions where we'd been hit. I worked on what we called hunter-killer teams in Vietnam. You went out with one other man. I went on five missions. Two missions I came back by myself. Lost two men . . .friends of mine.

Dr. Bellak: So that was still really on your mind.

Patient: This was why I felt . . .I had gotten to the point where I was afraid to love anybody, for the fear of losing them. In Nam, we got attached to each other very quick. All the guys I worked with. All the guys that worked with me. I knew things about them that I didn't know about my own brother, and they knew things about me. And after losing so many people, I just refused to get close to anybody . . .afraid to be close for fear of losing them.

Dr. Bellak: OK. Did you live all by yourself or did you see friends? From the time you and your wife separated. . .

Patient: Matter of fact, from the time I was strictly by myself. For the first three or four months.

I was from New Year's Eve till June 28th in the hospital. Just getting back together . . .about six months . . .had one leg cut off . . .that a mine blew off . . .I basically got back or got home and my wife and parents had already sort of set up the wedding arrangements. I didn't know about it.

Dr. Bellak: *But you knew the girl, I hope*₄.

Patient: Yeah, I knew the girl. *(Laughs)*.

Dr. Bellak: OK. *(Laughs)* I was thinking of some Japanese friends of mine where the mother selects the girl.

Patient: I went from 210 pounds down to 105 pounds, during a period of being in the hospital.

Dr. Bellak: In the hospital?

Patient: And there wasn't too much arguing. I didn't really want to fight or argue with anybody anymore. And I still basically stayed that way.

Dr. Bellak: They arranged it and you accepted it? Is that what you're telling me?

Patient: Yeah, we were good friends and we knew each other and had dated. Well, really only about a month before I went into the Army, but I would have postponed it awhile. Two or three months.

Dr. Bellak: Do I hear between the lines that if you had not been in your particular shape that you might not have agreed to the marriage?

Patient: More than likely, because when I was in the hospital I didn't even ask about it and they were talking about it then. They waited a year . . .she waited . . .we waited . . .to give me time to adjust to life and its problems.

Dr. Bellak: OK, so you agreed to go along with it, though. But what were your misgivings? What were your doubts?

Patient: Well, much of my life I had been very athletic. I ran track the first year I was in the Army. I had run cross-country. I didn't know if I could accept not running, not being able to go out and play. Basically, the thought of work . . .I could probably work as well as anybody, but I didn't know if I could do the other things in my life that always seemed to be so important to me.

Dr. Bellak: How did that affect the matter of whether you would or would not get married?

Patient: I basically didn't know if I wanted anybody else to support me that way and I wasn't sure that I even wanted to be that way.

Dr. Bellak: And then how did the marriage go?

---

4. This was probably a mostly inappropriate remark of mine, relieving my own tension. In part, it may have been constructive in pointing up — focusing on — the apparently excessively manipulating role of the patient's parents and wife.

Patient: Well, basically until the day I left, my wife felt that we had a great marriage. I usually agreed to whatever she wanted to do. *I really didn't want to argue for fear of being mad because I was afraid of what I might do if I got mad*₅. I just gave in and let her have her way. But it eventually just got to the point where *I started hating myself even more because I gave in to things* that I really didn't want to do, really didn't like.

Dr. Bellak: Could you give me some examples?

Patient: Well, like she was Catholic and I was Baptist. She never insisted that I go to Church, but she always wanted me to and I, basically, the times I did go . . .not really, I guess you'd say, under duress . . .but I really didn't want to go . . .But I got tired of saying no.

Dr. Bellak: Other things? How about the conflict between you two?

Patient: Well, basically, I liked to horseback ride and I liked athletic things. I still do. I like to water-ski and boat ride and every time I tried to get something that we could do together, she was always afraid of it. Like just horses. I bought two horses and she rode it about a hundred yards and stopped and she got thrown off it and she never would get back on it. It aggravated me that she would not try to do the things that we could do together. I just got to the point where I thought about what I wanted to do and just did it by myself.

Dr. Bellak: And towards the end, in July, what was the main point of the differences?

Patient: I had . . .we had drawn up blueprints for a house we were building and every time I would get through with them, she decided that she wanted to change things a little and we sent them back to the drawing board five times. And I started to agree with her, just not to argue and basically it wasn't the way I would have liked. I know about houses because I used to build them.

Dr. Bellak: Is that your field? What do you do?

Patient: A carpenter. I build furniture.

Dr. Bellak: That's what you still do?

Patient: As a hobby. I'm basically military retired.

Dr. Bellak: OK, what would you say ails you most right now?

Patient: *(Long pause)* Now I can never get to the point where I like me.

Dr. Bellak: OK, let's look into that. What is it, if you had to make a list, that makes you dislike yourself the most especially?

Patient: I'm very closed . . .I've just gotten passive. *(Starts to cry)* You know, that's not my way normally. Normally I speak out, right? I'm very straightforward.

Dr. Bellak: So you dislike yourself for that. Having given in.

5. This indicates another instance — among many — of the patient's fear of loss of impulse control. Clearly, his aggression turns promptly into intra-aggression.

Patient: It got to the point where *I didn't like me for giving in all the time*[6].

Dr. Bellak: OK, what else? Is that what *still* bothers you? Do you think about it?

Patient: Yeah.

Dr. Bellak: Today?

Patient: Yeah.

Dr. Bellak: Yesterday?

Patient: Yeah . . . Well, we didn't talk yesterday.

Dr. Bellak: Are you and your wife still on talking terms?

Patient: We're still on talking terms. I keep my kids on the weekend.

Dr. Bellak: But what of the things that you dislike about yourself kept running through your mind?

Patient: I guess part of it is the fear of me. Not being able to control me.

Dr. Bellak: And then what would you do?

Patient: Rather than be around people where I would be put into a position where I would be afraid that I would . . . I'd rather be by myself.

Dr. Bellak: I can understand that. But — and I know this is painful for you — but could you try and spell out specifically what you are afraid of? Of doing?

Patient: Disintegrating. Just accidentally becoming mad.

Dr. Bellak: And *then* what would you do?

Patient: Killing somebody out of instinct rather than . . .

Dr. Bellak: How? How?[7]

Patient: With my hands.

Dr. Bellak: How?

Patient: There are several methods that the Army taught us.

Dr. Bellak: Which ones did you think of using?

Patient: There are certain areas. Like the person's Adam apple. Taking your two hands and breaking off the windpipe. And several methods of crushing a man's ribcage and breaking his back. Hands over his neck, pull back. I had caught myself twice going for a man's throat when I had got angry.

Dr. Bellak: We want to understand. Could you be a little more graphic?

Patient: OK, the first time I was in a bar. Somebody else had come in *(sighs)* . . . he was a homesexual and made a proposition to me. And I got mad. If there weren't two guys in there that were friends of mine, and stopped me, I would have killed him.

---

6. This remark shows one of his many explicit and implicit references to his feelings of passivity.

7. Here I am attempting to get the situation as concrete as possible, to evoke emotions and to involve emotions in the patient's communication. I'm also inquiring in detail so that I can evaluate this man's potential for violence.

Dr. Bellak: How, in this case?

Patient: Well, I had grabbed him by his throat and had him up against the wall. I had my hands around his throat *(voice cracks)* and I was trying to ... And the other one. I had come into the bar and a man and another woman there were arguing and the man slapped her and I just went for him. I tried to kill him. I had him by the inside of his throat rather than the outside ... and this scared me to the point where I refused to get mad. That happened in the first year after coming back from the hospital. I got to the point where I just did not go out and socialize with people at all. I just basically stayed home.

Dr. Bellak: And has it become better now?

Patient: I have more control now. Of my feelings. I can take and block everything out. But also by blocking out, it leaves me in a situation where I have to fight myself.

Dr. Bellak: Well, you described that very clearly — that empty feeling that is left after you have tried to push away both love and hate. You made that very clear. Do you have friends at this point?

Patient: I have about four people that I trust enough to call a friend.

Dr. Bellak: Guys?

Patient: Three are male, one's a female.

Dr. Bellak: What did you dream last night?[8]

Patient: I don't remember if I had a dream. I only dreamed twice since I came back from Vietnam.

Dr. Bellak: Do you want to tell me those? Anytime that you feel too uncomfortable ...

Patient: One was four years ago when me and my wife separated for awhile. I guess it was the day after I had taken her back to Pittsburgh and left her with her parents. I took the train back. That night ... when I was in Nam I had gotten hit several times while I was sleeping and I had gotten into the habit of sleeping with a gun.

Dr. Bellak: By "hit" you mean attacked?

Patient: Yeah, while we were asleep. And I started dreaming about the day I was hit in Vietnam. For some reason, something made a noise in the house and I rolled out of bed and fired six times, blew six holes.

Dr. Bellak: In the dream?

Patient: No, really. And that was what scared me. I had rolled out of the bed. We were sleeping on cots in Vietnam and I always had an M16 there and here I had a .38 and when we got hit, I would roll out of the bed and start shooting. Before I really realized I was not still in Vietnam, I had

8. This is a very abrupt change of direction. At this point, I felt that I had obtained as much information as I could with regard to the precipitating factors. It is part of my conception of the guided interview that the therapist redirect it at times, even this abruptly.

rolled out of the bed and fired the gun six times till I flicked the trigger. And *I blew six holes in the side door of my house. Luckily there was nobody there.*[9]

Dr. Bellak: OK, that was the night after you left your wife off with her parents in . . .

Patient: Four years ago.

Dr. Bellak: And any others?

Patient: I had one while I was still in the hospital. Well, I had several of them that reoccurred as the same dream. It was the day we were hit, going through the minefield. The day I was hit I had 20 men on patrol . . . 20 men . . . seven of them were killed . . . and 12 of us came back amputees. Mutilated. One leg . . . both legs . . . both legs and arms. And the dream was about the same thing. About all the pain.

Dr. Bellak: *Do you recall any dreams from your childhood?*[10]

Patient: When I was real young — about being attacked by a big gorilla. A bunch of gorillas.

Dr. Bellak: Gorillas?

Patient: Being attacked by a bunch of gorillas. I think I had a habit of watching a lot of Tarzan movies. That dream really stuck with me.

Dr. Bellak: OK, that tells me a little bit. *You certainly have had a rough time.*[11] I just know a little bit about it. I'm still a consultant to West

9. At this point, it is necessary to evaluate the degree of likelihood of this man acting out on an impulse, either against himself or others. What should be kept in mind is:
   a. The patient had this dream and shot and emptied his pistol only *after* his wife had actually left the house. This fact leaves itself open to two interpretations:
      1. he acted only when he felt relatively safe that he would in fact not harm anyone, or
      2. the action might have been primarily motivated by anger over the wife's leaving the home
   b. All of the patient's acting out occurred when he had been drinking. In addition to advising him not to drink, the therapist also has a chance to use what in the text has been referred to as "sensitization to cues" or predicting in the hope of being wrong. The patient should be told that he is likely to feel enraged if he finds that somebody weak has been mistreated. One might eventually try to convey to him the concept of identification. Here one might also employ the intervention of mediate catharsis, to help this patient get rid of some of his rage over having been passive in some situations.
   At this point, one has to ask oneself again, "Just how dangerous is this man and should he be hospitalized?" We will have to look for further clues in the rest of the interview.
10. At this point, I make a somewhat abrupt inquiry again. Apropos of the dream, one should note the common denominator of being attacked, both in this childhood dream and in the dream about Viet Nam.
11. This remark is made to help in establishing a therapeutic alliance.

153

Point and I was during Vietnam so I saw quite a few people coming back and during World War II, I just had enough of a taste of it myself to know what you're talking about. Nothing quite that drastic.

Would you be kind enough and give me a very brief capsule of your life history?[12]

Patient: I was born in 1948. I'm 30 years old. I lived in . . . about until the time that I got drafted in the service.

Dr. Bellak: Your family?

Patient: I have an older brother, and an older sister, and a younger sister.

Dr. Bellak: How much older is your brother?

Patient: My brother is two years older than I am. My sister is six years older than I am, and my younger sister is six years younger than I am.

Dr. Bellak: And your parents? What kind of people are your parents?

Patient: They're basically, from anybody else's standpoint of view, very pleasant, easygoing people. Which my father is in reality. My mother likes to put on one face for everyone else and she really likes to bitch a lot.

Dr. Bellak: And what was her relation to you?

Patient: At times we had, or I had . . . problems growing up, where I had gotten into trouble doing certain things in school.

Dr. Bellak: Two terms that I don't understand. Problems growing up and getting into difficulties in school. What does that mean?

Patient: In school, I had always been passive, but twice I had gotten into trouble for fights.

Dr. Bellak: Passive meaning what?[13]

Patient: Easygoing. I didn't like to fight, didn't want to fight. Didn't want to argue. Didn't want to be a bully. Didn't — I tried to get along with people.

Dr. Bellak: I'll remind you of that later, OK?[13] But twice you got into fights?

Patient: And both times I felt that I was basically justified and then I was expelled from school.

Dr. Bellak: Did you hurt the guys?

Patient: Not so that they had to go to the hospital. Just two black eyes, that's all.

Dr. Bellak: OK *(Laughs)*. What was the worst thing your mother ever did to you?

Patient: That fight — that time I felt I was justified in getting into that fight, when I got home my father agreed with me, but yet my mother gave me a whipping for it.

Dr. Bellak: How did she whip you?

Patient: With a belt.

Dr. Bellak: How old were you at the time?

Patient: The first time probably 13. The second time about 15.

12. I make a change in direction again, to keep the interview efficient.
13. The patient has used the term "passive" several times now. I point it up to him at this point to prepare him for later interpretation.

154

Dr. Bellak: You were a pretty big guy.

Patient: Basically, it wasn't that she could hurt me by the whipping. Just so that she could hurt me inside. I leaned on her chair for her to do it. She didn't . . .

Dr. Bellak: She didn't what?

Patient: She didn't just whip me standing there. I basically . . .

*Dr. Bellak: So you sort of agreed to it.*₁₃

Patient: Yeah . . .

Dr. Bellak: Was it with your pants? You wore your pants?

*Patient: Without my pants.*₁₄

Dr. Bellak: If you would describe — *if you would apply three descriptive words to your father*₁₅, what would you pick?

Patient: (Silence).

Dr. Bellak: The first ones that come to your mind. Don't make it too hard.

Patient: Passive, in terms of my mother. In comparison. Strong. Outgoing in terms of everybody else.

Dr. Bellak: What does he do?

Patient: He's retired now.

Dr. Bellak: What did he do?

Patient: We had a grocery store in Pittsburgh. Then when we moved to Philly, he and my brother opened a construction company, which I worked with.

Dr. Bellak: And your mother? If you would describe her? You already said she was bitchy. What else?

Patient: Two-faced. She was one way outside to everybody else and another way inside. Incredible! She expected everyone to live one way and she wanted to live another way.

Dr. Bellak: You got through high school?

Patient: Yes.

Dr. Bellak: And then what did you do between that and the Army?

Patient: The time between high school and the time I was drafted . . . Well, I left home about six months before I graduated high school. The reason I left was that I had a fight with my father and he slapped me. That was the first time that he had beaten me up in five or six years. And I left because *I was afraid that I was going to hit him back. I wanted to hit him back . . . but I loved him. (Starts to cry)* I loved him but I wanted to hit him. *That's the reason I left.*₁₆

---

14. This small concrete detail of a 15-year-old boy being beaten on his naked behind speaks a volume concerning the family atmosphere and sadistic input, and the likely consequences for the patient's personality.

15. A tactic I often employ.

16. A situation repeated in the present, namely, now too the patient has a conflict between love and hate, and his use of the defense of withdrawal, which we see had been used earlier in his life with regard to his father.

Dr. Bellak: Why did he hit you?

Patient: We had that grocery store down there. We worked there together in the mornings. He had this habit of thinking that people were supermen. He'd tell you ten things that he wanted you to do, come back in five minutes, and think of two more things for you to do.

Dr. Bellak: I get the picture.

Patient: I think I was about 17. One day in the store I just finally told him that I couldn't take it anymore, that I only had two hands and not four hands. And that's the first time I think I ever talked back to him. And he slapped me.

Dr. Bellak: So that was a good time to get into the Army?

Patient: I worked for a year and a half for an oil company, after high school, and then I got drafted.

Dr. Bellak: Let's just think over some of the things that you've been saying.

Patient: Well, basically, what I didn't like about the way I was living was that I had gotten totally passive.

Dr. Bellak: If I can interrupt, if I may, I really didn't ask you enough about your wife. Would you just give me a very brief capsule. What kind of a woman is she?

Patient: My wife is 28, attractive. She has a different notion of what love is.

Dr. Bellak: What's her background? Let's stick to simple things.

Patient: Her background? After she got out of high school, she worked in a bank.

Dr. Bellak: What kind of family?

Patient: Her father is Italian, mother is German. And a lot of our problems stem from them because they never showed any love of any kind to her. They totally refuse — they ignore that sex exists. According to them, they don't know how kids are born, they just hatched them. She did not understand that. Her parents would never kiss in public or kiss openly or show any affection of any kind. Totally closed, cold, no feeling.

Dr. Bellak: If you were to describe how her parents are different from each other, what would you say?

Patient: Her father basically dominating, overbearing. Very tight with money. To the point where I know there were times when I have seen her younger brothers and sisters ask him for money, like a quarter to get a coke or something, he would never let anybody see what he had, he'd turn around and hide it and just take out a quarter.

Dr. Bellak: And her mother?

Patient: Her mother is like the father, basically, but not as aggressive.

Dr. Bellak: And your wife? If you could describe her briefly?

Patient: When we first got married, she was not basically aggressive. She was not aggressive in any way. She was afraid of any kind of sex. She really didn't know how to show affection. Just blocks it away.

Dr. Bellak: And did sex remain a problem?

Patient: Yes.

Dr. Bellak: Ordinarily, I would go into it, *but I don't think we need to under the circumstances.*[17]

But, now that you've rounded that out, did you mention children?

Patient: Yes, I have two girls.

Dr. Bellak: How old?

Patient: Five and almost two.

Dr. Bellak: How do you get along?

Patient: *(Sighs)* Both girls and me get along very well. I keep them every weekend — Friday and Saturday.

Dr. Bellak: OK, let's go back to *what you think we might have learned from what you have told me so far.*[18] After all, my job is, among other things, to be of help to you.

Patient: *(Silence)*.

Dr. Bellak: Well, let me make it a little bit easier. After all, I have a bit more perspective. It's easier for someone standing away. Also, I'm supposed to know something about it. Let's see if we can agree on some things. Look, what you complain about most and what brought you here is a fear that your anger might get out of hand and that you might do violence. And you have some very good reasons for it. Vietnam was a terrible experience. A couple of times it almost got out of hand and you had some very disturbing dreams, one of being hit and another in which you actually shot your .38.

Patient: Yeah, and in the other dream — well they were the same dream but it was when I was in the hospital.

Dr. Bellak: OK. Now, well curiously enough, when you told me your earlier history, particularly with school, you started off by saying that most of the time you were passive. Then a couple of times you beat up guys pretty badly. Your whole concern now, and about the marriage, was that you were being too passive. Feeling a great deal of anger, and the more you sat on it because you were afraid that it might get out of hand, the more you felt relief. As a kid, you had dreams of a gorilla going after you. And it scared you.

Patient: Yeah, terribly!

Dr. Bellak: In a way, I see a little similarity between that anxiety dream of somebody big, like a gorilla, doing you violence and the dreams of being hit, being attacked.

Patient: *Basically, they're both about being attacked.*[19]

17. I am referring to the public nature of the interview.
18. I'm preparing the patient for an interpretation, establishing a therapeutic alliance, and increasing the patient's awareness.
19. The patient is developing some insight.

Dr. Bellak: That's right.

Patient: They're both forms of being attacked. One by an animal and the other by a man.

Dr. Bellak: Yes. Whom did the gorilla look like, incidentally, in the dream? The first thing that comes to your mind.

Patient: A big ape.

Dr. Bellak: Is it anybody you know?

Patient: No.

Dr. Bellak: All right. *(Laughs)*.

Patient: Just looked like a big furry gorilla.

Dr. Bellak: So there is a certain continuity. While Vietnam undoubtedly made things worse . . .

Patient: The fear of being attacked. The thought of it.

Dr. Bellak: And also, the whole axis turns around aggression, passivity. In school, you say that you were passive most of the time, which is a curious way of putting it. Not everybody would put it that way. And that continues through your marriage, the closest relationship you have. You started out by saying, if I remember correctly, that when your parents arranged it, you were passive about it and agreed to the arrangement. When you described your wife, you said that she was not aggressive. That seems to be very much on your mind. You mentioned that she was not aggressive and then that she got to be and bugged you with the constant changes about the blueprints and different things. But at any rate, the point I want to make is that to be aggressive or to be passive seems to be a thread that runs through your head very readily. It's practically the main axis. Now, then, what did you tell me about your parents that might have a bearing on that?

Patient: Only that my father was passive with my mother.

Dr. Bellak: What effect might that have had on you? On your personality?

Patient: It made me where I almost did the same thing with my wife. Like the way my parents continuously argued.

Dr. Bellak: If I put it in my vulgar way, I would say that you might have said to yourself as a kid, "I'll be goddamed if I'm going to be a patsy to a woman the way my father has been." Is that right?

Patient: And I wound up doing the same thing. Either that, or I let myself get to the point of doing the same thing.

Dr. Bellak: Either that, or at least it felt that way to you.

Patient: Right.

Dr. Bellak: What conclusions would you draw?

Patient: That I'm afraid of being like my father. Afraid of being pushed.

Dr. Bellak: OK, could I *push*[20] that just a bit? That you're afraid of being

20. This is a very ill-advised choice of word by me!

passive. One of the guys who got to you particularly was a homosexual in the bar.

Patient: Yeah. But I was only 21 at the time. I never had relations with another man. Never wanted to. Never . . .

Dr. Bellak: So, if I may stretch things a little by implication — the idea that he would think that you would be in any way interested in something not masculine got you sore. That's the point I want to make for right now. And how do you think we could fit in that other time that you nearly got at the guy's Adam's apple?

Patient: That was over a man striking a woman. I was brought up never to do that.

Dr. Bellak: Well, aside from the fact that . . . psychologically, what do you think it might be? Look, you saw somebody attacked. When you and I see a car accident on the highway, what do we do?[21]

Patient: Stop and see if we can help.

Dr. Bellak: But if there is already an ambulance and a cop car there, what do we do anyhow?

Patient: Stop and see if anybody is huⅰt.

Dr. Bellak: Yes, but usually everyone slows down a bit because you feel that "Gee, this could happen to me. Maybe I shouldn't drive so fast." One identifies, as we psychiatrists say, with the other person. Could there have been something in that, when you saw the guy hit the woman?

Patient: Other than the actual fact?

Dr. Bellak: Well, I could be wrong, but what I wonder about in such a case, if one doesn't identify with the underdog. You don't want to see her hit, because you feel, "Damn, I don't want to be hit."

Patient: I don't want to be hurt, but I don't want to hurt anyone either.

Dr. Bellak: OK, let's see if we can agree on a couple of things. One is that Vietnam was a terrible experience. It might do all sorts of things to anybody's . . .

Patient: (interrupts) People have to do a lot of things that they shouldn't have to do.

Dr. Bellak: I know, but this might just have made more of an impression on *your* personality because you had already been concerned with a fear of being attacked, as witnessed in the dreams about the gorilla, a recurrent dream in your childhood. You felt that you had to stand up against your mother, about whom you had understandably mixed feelings. Mixed feelings. You bent over the chair and let her whip you, but at the same time you must have been full of a hell of a rage.

Patient: Anger, because I didn't understand why. I felt that I was justified in what I did.

21. I attempted to convey the concept of identification, but failed completely.

Dr. Bellak: Well, among other things . . . So that you came with that **pattern**. Vietnam made it worse. Then you had the feeling that you let yourself be shoved into a marriage. You started out with a bit of a grudge and misgivings that you had let yourself be shoved. And then, very promptly, saw yourself in a situation and a relationship that seemed too much like the one you saw between your father and mother.

What does it add up to? *If you and I would just change chairs mentally and you were the psychiatrist, what would you think of all the things you have heard today?*[22]

Patient: As far as the marriage?

Dr. Bellak: No, as far as understanding what is going on with you.

Patient: What's going on with me?

Dr. Bellak: Yes, and what we might do about it.

Patient: (Silence).

Dr. Bellak: Well, in view of the fact that we see that some of the same problems that trouble you now and troubled you in your marriage existed in some form in your youth, in your earlier life, what do you think you and your therapist might work on?

Patient: Getting me to the point that I can, basically, release enough of myself to feel.

Dr. Bellak: How do you propose to do that?

Patient: The only way I can do it is to learn not to be afraid of reaching out and of being hurt.

Dr. Bellak: Is there another way? Obviously, what ails you now has its origins in childhood. Getting to understand the fact that many of the things that happened to you as a kid make Vietnam much more difficult for you to absorb and digest and to deal with now — and they still have an effect on you today, the things that happened to you as a child. The better you can understand to a certain extent how you either overemphasize or even distort some of the things that happen to you now because you were already primed in childhood — the gorillas and all that — the less you are going to feel that rage. I think that rage has been there since childhood, and got an extra shove from all the things in Vietnam. I don't know if you could have married any woman . . .

Patient: At that point.

Dr. Bellak: At any time, and not come with the same set of expectations. "I better watch out that she is not a battle-axe who shoves me around." Because that is what you were accustomed to. So, the more you work on that, on understanding your current feelings in terms of your early past, with Vietnam just thrown in psychologically for good measure, the better able you will be to handle the tensions that you have, which just

22. This is often a useful strategy for increasing insight.

seem to be all along a matter of passivity, aggression — really, apparently, the axis around which your life revolves. Some people have that problem even without Vietnam if one has had that childhood. That's one thing. The more you can go into that, the better.

Would you like to hear my guess about who the gorilla was in the dream? I bet you can make a pretty good guess. Can you tell me? The first person *who comes to your mind.*

Patient: My mother.[23]

Dr. Bellak: Oh, sure. And I bet if we could go into the dream in enough detail we could find things that would identify her. And I think that she is even sometimes identified in your mind with some of the Vietnamese.* Well, it gets a bit complex. But those are some of the things that you two can continue to go into. Meanwhile, I'm sure you use whatever athletics you can to get rid of some of the tension. I think that's a very good short range measure. Like punching a bag.

You're right-handed, I take it.

Patient: Yes.

Dr. Bellak: Never were left-handed?**

Patient: No.

Dr. Bellak: Well, I think that's probably as much as we can go into now. I feel having seen problems similar to yours before, that there is a good deal of hope that the two of you — you and your therapist — can really work this out.

You know, there's not anyone so tough that he doesn't have some passivity. I don't care how tough the guy is.

Patient: Basically, I'm not afraid of being passive. The problem is that usually I get too passive.

Dr. Bellak: Well, in part I guess you had to because with your mother . . . and then that made you feel like nothing and you had to get really angry. So, if you two can work it out so that you neither feel too passive nor the need to feel too aggressive, I think that things should work out very well.

Thank you very much again. I really appreciate that you were willing to discuss things.

Patient: Thank you very much.

---

*   The ideal concise interpretation I should have made here is: "I think all you did was to replace the *gorillas* with *guerillas.*"

**   This was just a brief notion that the patient's problems with impulse control might be related to any aspect of minimal brain dysfunction. I discuss this more fully in another book (1).

23.   The discussion seems to have decreased repression and increased awareness.

REFERENCE

1. Bellak, L. Adult psychiatric states with MBD and their ego function assessment. In L. Bellak (Ed.), *Psychiatric Aspects of Minimal Brain Dysfunction in Adults.* New York: Grune & Stratton, 1979.

REFERENCES

1. Ackerman, N. W. *Treating the Troubled Family*. New York: Basic Books, 1966.

2. Bellak, L. The concept of projection: An experimental investigation and study of the concept. *Psychiatry*. 7:353-370, 1944.

3. Bellak, L. The emergency psychotherapy of depression. In: *Specialized Techniques in Psychotherapy*. Edited by G. Bychowski and J. L. Despert. New York: Basic Books, 1952. pp. 323-336.

4. Bellak, L. Free association: Conceptual and clinical aspects. *Int. J. of Psycho-Anal*. 42:9-20, 1961.

5. Bellak, L. Depersonalization as a variant of self-awareness. In: *Unfinished Tasks in the Behavioral Sciences*. Edited by A. Abrams. Baltimore, Williams & Wilkins, 1964.

6. Bellak, L. The concept of acting out: Theretical considerations. In: *Acting Out - Theoretical and Clinical Aspects*. Edited by L. Abt & S. Weissman. New York: Grune & Stratton, 1965.

7. Bellak, L. *The Thematic Apperception Test, Children's Apperception Test, and Senior Apperception Technique in Clinical Use*. Third and revised edition. New York: Grune & Stratton, 1975.

8. Bellak, L. (Editor and Contributor) *Psychiatric Aspects of Minimal Brain Dysfunction in Adults*. New York: Grune & Stratton, 1979.

9. Bellak, L. Editorial: Point of view: Ventilation is not enough. *Roche Report. Frontiers of Psychiatry*. Edited by H. Henderson. 10:14, 1980

10. Bellak, L. & Antell, M. Understanding the depressed. A review of Edith Jacobson's Depression: Comparative Studies of Normal, Neurotic and Psychotic Conditions. *Contemporary Psychology*. 19:364-365, 1974.

11. Bellak, L. & Baker, S. *Reading Faces*. Holt, Rinehart & Winston, 1981. Soft cover: Bantam Press, 1982.

12. Bellak, L. (with P. Faithorn). *Crises and Special Problems in Psychoanalysis and Psychotherapy*. New York: Brunner/Mazel, 1980.

12A. Bellak, L. & Goldsmith, L. (Editors) *The Broad Scope of Ego Function Assessment*. New York: John Wiley & Sons, 1983. (In Press)

13. Bellak, L. & Haselkorn, F. Psychological aspects of cardiac illness and rehabilitation. *Social Casework*. 37:483-489, 1956.

14. Bellak, L., Hurvich, M. & Gediman, H. *Ego Functions in Schizophrenics, Neurotics, and Normals*. New York: John Wiley & Sons, 1973.

15. Bellak, L. & Jacques, E. On the problem of dynamic conceptualization in case studies. *Character Pers*. 1:20-39, 1942.

16. Bellak, L., Meyer E. J., Rosenberg, S., & Zuckerman, M. An experimental study of brief psychotherapy. In: *An Evaluation of the Results of the Psychotherapies*. Edited by S. Lesse. Charles C. Thomas, Springfield, Illinois, 1968.

17. Bellak, L. & Meyers B. Ego function assessment and analysability. *The International Review of Psycho-Analysis*. 2:413-427, 1975.

18. Bellak, L., Prola, M., Meyer, E. J., & Zuckerman, M. Psychiatry in the medical-surgical emergency clinic. *Arch. Gen. Psychiatry*. 10:267-269, 1964.

19. Bellak, L. & Small, L. *Emergency Psychotherapy and Brief Psychotherapy*. New York: Grune & Stratton, 1978.

20. Bibring, E. The mechanism of depression. In: *Affective Disorders*. Edited by P. Greenacre. New York: International Universities Press, 1953.

21. Cannon, W. B. *Bodily Changes in Panic, Hunger, Fear and Rage*. New York: Appleton, Second Edition, 1929.

22. Davenloo, H. *Basic Principles and Techniques in Short-term Dynamic Psychotherapy*. New York: Spectrum, 1978.

23. English, H. B. & English, A. C. *A Comprehensive Dictionary of Psychological and Psychoanalytic Terms*. New York, London, and Toronto: Longmans Green, 1958.

24. Fenichel, O. *The Psychoanalytic Theory of Neurosis.* New York: W. W. Norton & Company, 1945.

25. Freud, A. *The Ego and the Mechanisms of Defense.* New York: International Universities, 1936.

26. Friedman, P. & Linn, L. Some psychiatric notes on the *Andrea Doria* disaster. *Amer. J. Psychiatry.* 114:426-432, 1957.

27. Glover, E. (1930) Grades of ego differentiation. In: *On the Early Development of the Mind.* New York: International Universities Press, 1956.

28. Hartmann, H. *Ego Psychology and the Problem of Adaptation* (1939). Reprinted New York: International Universities, 1964.

29. Hilberman, E. *The Rape Victim.* Washington, D. C. American Psychiatric Association, 1976.

30. Hinsie, L. E. & Campbell, R. J. *Psychiatric Dictionary.* Third Edition. New York: Oxford University Press, 1960.

31. Jacobson, E. *Depression: Comparative Studies of Normal, Neurotic, and Psychotic Conditions.* New York: International Universities Press, 1971.

32. Jacobson, G. F., Strickler, M. & Morley, M. E. Generic and individual approaches to crisis intervention. *Am. J. Public Health.* 58:2, 1968.

33. James, W. (1918) *The Principles of Psychology.* Volume II. Dover Publications, 1950.

34. Jones, E. *The Life and Work of Sigmund Freud.* Volume II. New York: Basic Books, 1955.

35. Leighton, A. H. *An Introduction to Social Psychiatry.* Springfield, Illinois, Charles C. Thomas, 1960. p. 110.

36. Lewin, B. *The Psychoanalysis of Elation.* W. W. Norton, New York, 1950.

37. Lindemann, E. Symptomatology and management of acute grief. *Am. J. Psychiatry.* 101:141-148, 1944.

38. Malan, D. H. *The Frontier of Brief Psychotherapy: An Example of the Convergence of Research and Clinical Practice*. New York: Plenum Medical Book Co., 1976.

39. Mann, J. *Time Limited Psychotherapy*. Cambridge, Mass., Harvard Univ. Press, 1973.

40. Marañon, G. The psychology of gesture. *J. of Nerv. and Ment. Disease*. 122:469-497, 1950.

41. Minuchin, S. *Families and Family Therapy*. Cambridge, Mass: Harvard University Press, 1974.

42. Oberndorf, C. P. *A History of Psychoanalysis in America*. New York: Grune & Stratton, 1953.

43. Parad, H. J. (Editor) *Crisis Intervention: Selected Reading*. New York: Family Service Association of America, 1967.

44. Pinner, M. & Miller, B. (Editors) *When Doctors are Patients*. New York: W. W. Norton, 1952.

45. Pollock, G. *On Freud's Psychotherapy of Bruno Walter*. Annual of Psychoanalysis, Volume III, 1975.

46. Rapaport, D. Present-day ego psychology (1956) In: *The Collected Papers of David Rapaport*. Edited by M. Gill. New York: Basic Books, 1967.

47. Rosen, J. *Direct Psychoanalytic Psychiatry*. New York: Grune & Stratton, 1962.

48. Rosen, V. H. Psychiatric problems in general surgery. In: *Psychology of Physical Illness*. Edited by L. Bellak. New York: Grune & Stratton, 1952.

49. Rosenberg, S., Prola, M., Meyer, E. J., Zuckerman, M. & Bellak, L. Factors related to improvement in brief psychotherapy. In: *An Evaluation of the Results of the Psychotherapies*. Edited by S. Lesse. Charles C. Thomas, Springfield, Illinois, 1968.

50. Schultz, C. G. Self and object differentiation as a measure of change in psychotherapy. In: *Psychotherapy of Schizophrenia*. Edited by J. G. Gunderson & L. R. Mosher. New York: Jason Aranson, 1975.

51. Shneidman, E. Suicide notes reconsidered. *Psychiatry*. 36:379-394, 1973.

52. Shneidman, E. Psychotherapy with suicidal patients. In: *Specialized Techniques in Individual Psychotherapy.* Edited by B. Karasu & L. Bellak. New York: Brunner/Mazel, 1980.

53. Shneidman, E. & Farberow, N. L. Clues to suicide. *Public Health Reports.* 71:109-114, 1956.

54. Sifneos, P. *Short-term Psychotherapy and Functional Crisis.* Cambridge, Mass., Harvard University Press, 1972.

55. Trainor, D. MHP said to be responsive to pimozide therapy. *Psychiatry News.* August 1, 1980.

Note: Throughout the text a number of technical, usually psychoanalytic, terms have been used which are probably well-known to all the readers. If there are some exceptions, please consult *A Glossary of Psychoanalytic Terms and Concepts.* The American Psychoanalytic Association. Edited by B. E. Moore and B. D. Fine. New York, Second Edition, 1968.

Subject Index

Achievement, need for, 2
Acting out, 42, 46, 60-66, 68, 69, 70, 71, 73, 115, 141, 153
Acute psychotic states, see Psychosis
Adaptive regression in the service of the ego (ARISE), 25, 26
ADD, see Attention Deficit Disorder
Administrative aspects, 7, 12-14, 80
Affective disorders, 57
   see also Hypomanic; Depression
Agoraphobia, see Phobia
Aggression, 17, 21, 30, 40, 45, 46, 52, 53, 54, 65, 71, 72, 83, 91, 101, 103, 105, 108, 109, 112, 113, 118, 120, 126, 130, 131, 137, 140, 141-143, 150
Alcoholism, 2, 22
Anamnesis, 9, 16, 17, 20, 69, 126
Anhedonia, 147
Anxiety, 4, 20, 21, 23, 27, 38, 47, 66, 73, 79, 81, 82, 83, 89, 93, 94, 95, 97, 99, 101, 102, 103, 109, 110, 114, 115, 116, 128, 132, 133, 134, 139, 140, 141, 142, 143, 144, 157
   Anxiety Arousing Therapy, 2
   anxiety attack, 8, 21, 115
   anxiety hysteria, 117-126,
      see also Phobia
   castration, 3, 97, 100, 102, 115, 125, 132
   examination, 118
Apperceptive distortion, 3, 28, 39, 54, 105, 132
Attention Deficit Disorder, (ADD), 22, 62, 66, 89
Autonomous function, 25, 26
Auxiliary ego, see Ego
Auxiliary reality testing, see Reality testing
Avoidance, 89

Bedwetting, 11, 12, 21
Behavioral therapy, 3, 5, 30
Behavior modification, 3
Bereavement, 11, 106, 112-113
Borderline, 26, 125

Castration anxiety, see Anxiety, castration
Catharsis and Mediate Catharsis, 18, 30, 44, 45, 53, 57, 63, 64, 71, 80, 97, 106, 107, 110, 129, 134, 141-153
Chief complaint, 20
   history of, 20, 21
   secondary complaints, 21

Claustrophobia, see Phobia
Cognitive approach, 3
Competence, see Mastery-Competence
Conditioning, 42, 123
Conjoint therapy, 2, 10, 17, 30, 33, 44, 47, 50, 81
Counter-phobic symbols and defenses, see Phobia
Countertransference, 27, 81, 101
Crisis intervention, 10

Death, 54, 69, 71, 74, 131
   death-defying, 113
   death wishes, 120
   fears of, 96, 99-100, 101, 102, 103, 106, 108, 112-113, 121, 122
   see also Bereavement
Defenses, 4, 5, 12, 22, 24, 26, 53, 56, 57, 88, 91, 93, 102, 107, 114, 124, 139, 140, 143, 153
   see also under individual defense
Defensive functions, 25, 26
Denial, 11, 51, 53, 57, 89, 93, 101, 102, 103, 107, 110, 112, 115, 129, 133, 140
Depersonalization, 24, 54, 108, 130, 135-145
   endogenous, 50, 57
   reactive, 50, 57
Derealization, 24, 130
Diagnosis, 22, 68, 84, 101, 102, 139
Displacement, 111
Dissociative process, 28
Draw-A-Person Test, 98
Dreams, 12, 27, 28, 32, 33, 39, 97, 105, 115, 140, 152-153, 157-158, 159, 161
Drive repression, 30, 44, 46
Drugs, 5, 14, 16, 17, 18, 30, 44, 47, 50, 63, 65, 66, 70, 73-74, 78, 83-84, 87, 91
   and panic, 128, 130
   and unreality, 137, 139, 142, 143-144, 145
   drug dependence, 2
   for phobias, 119, 123-124
   see also Medication
Dyadic Therapy, 12, 17, 30, 33, 50, 51, 58-59, 73, 81

ECT, see Electroconvulsive Therapy
Education, 3, 37, 40, 44, 46, 56, 94, 96, 98, 101, 143, 144
Ego, 22, 23, 90, 134, 137, 139, 141
   auxiliary, 23, 53, 54
   ego ideal, 23, 54
   ego strength, 71

Ego function assessment, 23, 27
  ego functions and their compo-
    nents, 24-27, 83
Elevator phobia, see Phobia
Erythrophobia, see Phobia
Electroconvulsive Therapy, 74
Evaluation, 32
Exhibitionism, 20, 21, 120, 137,
  141-143

Family history, 19, 21-22, 69, 70, 72
Family network therapy, 44, 47, 80-81
Family sessions, 10, 17, 30, 33, 50
Fear of flying or driving, see Phobia
Free association, 39, 42

Guilt, 100, 107, 109, 112, 114, 122, 130

History-taking, 9, 20, 21, 27, 29, 105,
  120
Homicidal, 10, 78, 79
Hospitalization, 8, 12, 16, 18, 63, 66,
  70, 73-74, 78, 79-80, 82, 87, 91, 109,
  130, 153
Hypomanic, 55
  and manic, 56
Hysterical personality, 62, 139, 140
  hysteria, 114

Identification, 28, 45, 97, 108, 112,
  121, 131, 153, 159
Insight, 2, 3, 5, 21, 28, 33, 34, 37, 41,
  42, 47, 53, 54, 55, 97, 121, 123, 133,
  139, 157, 160
Insight psychotherapy, 3, 5, 33
Intake, 13
Intellectualization, 44, 46
Internalization, therapeutic, 14, 17, 18,
  28, 29, 30, 37, 38, 40, 41, 44, 45, 53,
  55, 57, 63, 64, 66, 71, 78, 83, 87, 88,
  89, 97, 101, 105, 107, 109, 115, 122,
  124, 128, 131, 140, 141, 144, 154, 157,
  161
Interview, sample of initial, 147-161
Intra-aggression, 30, 51, 52, 53-54, 72,
  147, 150
Introject, Introjection, 4, 45, 52, 53,
  57, 71, 101

James-Lange theory, 134
Judgement, 24, 26, 90, 113, 114, 132

Learning theory, 2
Life events, catastrophic, 104-116
Life history, see History-taking

Manic, and hypomanic, 55, 56, 57, 88,
  89, 130

Manic-depressive disorder, 22
Mastery-competence, 25, 26
Mediate catharsis, see Catharsis and
  Mediate
Medication, 14, 16, 47, 83, 98, 143
  see also Drugs
Migratory Phobia, see Phobia
Minimal Brain Dysfunction, 68, 161
  see also Attention Deficit Disorder
Multiple personality, 141

Narcissism, 51, 56-57, 58, 97, 98, 108,
  139
  narcissistic attachment, 24
  narcissistic behavior, 40
  secondary narcissism, 56
Neurosis, 1, 8, 25, 26, 27, 39, 61, 97,
  110, 115, 130, 139
  see also Obsessive; Success
    neurosis; Phobia

Object constancy, 24
Object relations theory, 4, 23
  object relations, 24, 26, 51, 54, 55,
    57, 58-59, 112, 139, 140
  anaclitic, 56, 58, 139
Object representations, 4, 52
Obsessive, 17, 21, 61, 68, 124, 125,
  126, 142
Omnipotence, 17, 64

Pan phobia, see Phobia
Panic, 3, 4, 12, 17, 21, 42, 46, 68, 70,
  71, 73, 88, 90, 93, 114, 116, 118,
  127-134, 143
  endogenous, 128, 130, 132
  exogenous, 128, 131, 132
  mixed, 128
Panic attack, 10
Paranoid, 55, 62, 66, 68, 88, 98, 100,
  124
Phobia, 61, 110, 117-125
  agoraphobia, 2, 20, 21, 118, 120, 139
  claustrophobia, 115, 118, 120, 121,
    122, 125
  counter-phobic symbols and
    defenses, 120, 124
  elevator phobia, 121
  erythrophobia, 21
  fear of driving, 118, 120
  fear of flying, 121, 122
  migratory phobia, 124
  pan-phobia, 125
  school phobia, 20, 120
Physical illness, Surgery, 92-103

Prevention
  primary, 5, 7, 11, 12
  secondary, 5, 7, 11, 12
  tertiary, 5, 7, 12
Primal scene, 2, 11, 114, 125
Primal scream, 45, 107
Primitiveness, 24, 70, 71
Projection, 53, 102, 138, 144
Projective techniques, 37, 40, 98
  see Thematic Apperception Test
  (TAT); Rorschach; Draw-A-Person
  Test
Psychotic, 1, 8, 12, 22, 23, 26, 27,
  75-84, 94, 95, 98, 100, 128, 129, 130,
  132, 139, 142
  acute psychotic states, 62, 66, 71,
  76, 83, 85-91
  see also Schizophrenia

Rape, 11, 105, 106, 109, 110, 114-115
Reality testing, 24, 26, 71, 83, 90, 126,
  132
  auxiliary, 44, 45, 66
Regression, 79, 80, 82, 108, 120
Regulation and control of drives, 24,
  26
Repression, 46, 97, 102, 107, 133, 141,
  147, 161
  see also Drive repression
Resistance, 7, 13, 14, 147
Rorschach blots, 40

Schizophrenia, 12, 22, 25, 68, 89, 125,
  143
School phobia, see Phobia
Secondary gains, 29, 30, 79, 80, 96,
  97-98
Secondary narcissism, see
  Narcissism, secondary
Self-esteem, 2, 14, 24, 30, 51, 52, 53,
  54, 56, 57, 58, 62, 108, 109, 110, 111
Self-identity, 24
Self-representations, 4, 23, 52, 54
Sense of reality, 24, 26
Sensitization to signals, Signal
  awareness, 44, 46, 63, 65
Separation, 34, 137, 141-143
Separation anxiety, 2, 20, 33, 130
Significant other, 59, 70, 73, 87, 90
Splitting, 140, 141

Stimulus barrier, 25, 26
Success neurosis, 22, 66, 130
Suicidal, Suicide, 10, 11, 22, 50, 52,
  64, 65, 67-74, 78, 79, 90, 115
Superego, 21, 22, 23, 30, 45, 51, 52, 53,
  54, 63, 65, 68, 71, 89, 112, 130, 141
Support, 1, 44, 46-47, 72, 90, 93, 94, 99,
  101, 105, 110, 115, 133
Supportive therapy, 5
Suppression, 107
Surgery, 11, 92-103, 126
Symbiotic-object choice, 24
  relationships, 58, 130, 139, 145
Symptoms, 4, 5, 6, 7, 8, 10, 12, 32, 39,
  76, 89, 91, 93, 107, 124, 126, 134, 140,
  145
Synthetic-integrative functions, 25,
  26, 32, 33
Systems theory, Systems approach, 2,
  3, 5, 17, 21, 51, 58-59

TAT, see Thematic Apperception Test
Termination, 27, 32, 33, 34
  spontaneous conclusion, 29
Thematic Apperception Test (TAT), 28,
  98
Therapeutic alliance, 9, 19, 27-29, 30,
  33, 38, 46, 98, 153, 157
Therapeutic contract, 9, 19, 29-30
Therapeutic neutrality, 34, 38, 70, 72,
  73
Thought disorder, 47, 66
Thought processes, 24, 26
Transference, 19, 27, 28, 29, 41, 52, 53,
  54, 55, 58, 62, 71, 123
  negative, 27
  neurosis, 61
  paranoid, 27
  positive, 27, 32, 34, 35, 58
  psychosis, 81
  sexualized, 27

Undoing, 21
Unreality, feelings of, 135-145
  see also Sense of Reality;
    Depersonalization; Derealization

Working through, 33, 37, 41-42, 52, 53,
  54, 55, 58, 74, 100, 109, 110, 112, 113,
  114, 115, 119, 123, 133, 142, 145

Name Index

Bellak, L., 25, 26, 103; as interviewer, 147-161
Bibring, E., 53
Boltzman, 107

Campbell, R. J., 61
Cannon, W. B., 134

Davenloo, H., 2, 41

English, A. C., 61
English, H. B., 61

Farberow, N. L., 72
Friedman, P., 105
Freud, Anna, 4
Freud, S., 4, 38, 107, 141

Gediman, H., 25, 26
Glover, E., 141

Hartmann, H., 4
Haselkorn, F., 103
Helmholtz, 107
Hilberman, E., 105, 114
Hinsie, L. E., 61
Hurvich, M., 25, 26

Jacobson, Edith, 52, 54, 57, 130

Jacobson, G. F., 108
James-Lange, 134

Leighton, A. H., 13
Lewin, B., 56, 57, 69, 71
Lindemann, E., 109, 115
Linn, L., 105

Mahler, Gustav, 4
Malan, D. H., 2
Mann, J., 2
Marañon, G., 134
Morley, M. E., 108
Munro, Alistair, 126

Oberndorf, C. P., 35

Rapaport, D., 23
Rosen, J., 80

Schultz, C. G., 142
Shneidman, E., 68, 72, 73
Sifneos, P., 2
Stein, Gertrude, 110
Strickler, M., 108

Walter, Bruno, 4
Wylie, Phillip, 118, 120